NOTES

UPON

THE PENAL LAW

OF

𝔗𝔥𝔢 𝔓𝔯𝔬𝔱𝔢𝔰𝔱𝔞𝔫𝔱 𝔈𝔭𝔦𝔰𝔠𝔬𝔭𝔞𝔩 𝔆𝔥𝔲𝔯𝔠𝔥.

WITH A

DRAFT OF A GENERAL CANON,

BY MURRAY HOFFMAN, ESQ.

Nulli Sacerdotum liceat ignorare Canones.--*Cœlestinus* 1.

WIPF & STOCK · Eugene, Oregon

Wipf and Stock Publishers
199 W 8th Ave, Suite 3
Eugene, OR 97401

Notes Upon The Penal Law of the Protestant Episcopal Church
With a Draft of a General Canon
By Hoffman, Murray
ISBN 13: 978-1-62564-879-2
Publication date 4/22/2014
Previously published by Wm C. Bryant, 1853

NOTES UPON

THE PENAL LAW OF THE CHURCH.

The subject of the administration of the discipline of the Church has engaged the attention of her members, within the last few years, to a great extent.

A feeling of marked dissatisfaction with our present system prevails; a dissatisfaction strong in proportion to the number of cases in which it has been tried. This unquiet and distrustful spirit exists chiefly among the clergy, for whose government and protection a code is principally requisite.

Much of this imperfection may be attributed to a cause which in itself is a blessing. Every code of retributive law springs from the errors or the crimes of men; and the administration of justice becomes more comprehensive and more clearly defined, as experience developes the inefficiency of previous regulations. The occasions to enforce the discipline of the church have happily been rare. But the great increase of the number of her members increases the probability of offences, and more and more exhibit the deficiencies of the system.

As long ago as the year 1835 some of the most sagacious of our churchmen appreciated and deplored this evil, and measures were suggested to correct it. (a.) The subject deserves an earnest and patient investigation; and should call forth a resolution to dispose of it comprehensively, and upon fixed principles. The author presents his humble offering of labour and reflection, to assist perhaps in the accomplishment of a work of such deep moment.

It will not be uninteresting or irrelevant to collect some historical notices of the judicial system in the ancient church.

(a.) Hawke's Const. and Canons, p. 34,

The earliest records of the Jewish church warrant the belief, that in the patriarchal ages, the power of judging resided in the heads of families, and the chiefs of tribes.

Under the Mosaic law, the original, and subsequently the principal authority was vested in Moses during his life. In consequence of the advice of his father-in-law, he instructed the people to choose judges, rulers of thousands, rulers of hundreds, &c. These decided the causes of the people at all seasons, bringing however the hard cases unto Moses. (a.)

This direction is renewed in Deuteronomy; (cap. xvi. v. 18,) and thus the judicial arrangement, as to secular cases at least, was established.

There was, however, either by appeal or originally, an authority in the priesthood associated in some instances with the judge. (Deut. xvii. 8–13; ibid cap. xxi. 1.)

In this last passage we find the Judges and the Elders contra-distinguished; (b) and in numerous passages we find the phrase " Elders" used in a manner which indicates a distinct class, not merely seniors in age. (Joshua, cap. xxviii. 31; 2 Sam. xix. 11; 2 Chron. cap. v. 2; ibid, xix. 8.) The last passage is important. It recognises the separation of the judicial power, in the appointment of judges for all the cities, city by city, (generally allowed to be for civil matters;) and investing or recognizing in the Priests, Levites, and Chief of the Fathers of Israel, a power for other matters. It is declared that Amaziah, the chief Priest, was over the people in all matters of the Lord, and Zebediah, of the house of Judah, for all the King's matters. I do not know of an earlier record, in which the distinction between ecclesiastical and civil subjects of judgment, and the division of the authority to judge them, is to be found.

But it is an admitted fact in Jewish History, that the Great Sanhedrim became the chief council, exercising for a long series of

---

(a.) Exodus, xviii. 18.

(b.) "If one be found slain in the land, lying in the field, and it be not known who hath slain him, then the Elders and the Judges shall come forth, &c."

Rabbi Ben Jacob says upon this passage, that the Elders here mean the Great Sanhedrim, and the Judges the King and High Priest. (Apud Selden *De Synedriis Ebraeorum.*)

years the highest judicial office, and its members were *the elders* (*Presbyteroi*,) and Scribes (*a*).

I have regarded the question of the composition and authority of the Sanhedrim as of so much interest, as to obtain from the kindness of an eminent and learned Rabbi, a valuable statement in reply to some questions addressed to him. (*b*) He says, "According to Jewish tradition, the council of elders, *Gerousia* or *Sanhedrin*, founded by Moses, was a permanent body, composed of a president and seventy members, which filled up its own vacancies. The chain of uninterrupted succession, with the names of the presidents or chiefs, is preserved in the Mishua treatise Aboth ' of the fathers.' It begins with Moses, and is carried to the second generation after the destruction of Jerusalem by Titus. The French Monk, Calmet, however, and after him most modern Christian writers, deny this tradition, and assign a much later date to the institution of the Sanhedrin. From Josephus not speaking of that body until the reign of Hyrcan I. they deem themselves justified in looking upon it as of, then, recent origin. But independent of scriptural evidence, which proves the existence of a body or council of seventy elders, not only during the first, but also during the early part of the second temple, we find such a body repeatedly mentioned in the Books of the Maccabees, which are confessedly older than Josephus, and which, though not canonical, are entitled to belief as historical evidence. Upon the whole we may fairly assume that though under such a King as Solomon and most of his successors, the power and influence of the council were very circumscribed, yet the body itself never ceased to exist.

(*a*) Mr. Selden quotes a passage from Maimonides, which he thus translates: " Parile jus spectat ad synedrium magnum et ad synedrium quodlibet minus, et ad Forum Triumvirale, in hoc scilicet, ut oportet quemlibet eorum qui in illa cooptantur creari per manus impositionem ab alio, qui sic ante creatum fuerit; ut Moses magister ita creavit Jehosiam, sicut quod scripta est, *et manus suas ei imposuit*, et fecit eum Rabbinum—atque ita Septuaginta Presbyteros creavit Moses, et residit super eos Majestas Divina, et Presbyteri illi alios similiter creabant, aliique alios. Et compertum est sic creatum fuisse alium ab alio, usque in tempora Domus Judicii Mosis." Selden *De Synedriis Veterorum Ebraeorum.* Lib. 1, Cap. 14, p. 303.

Grotius says: "Apud Judaeos mansit sceptrum in Magno Synedrio etiam post confiscationem Archelai. Apud Selden de Sanhedriis, 414.

(*b*) Doctor Raphael of New York. See in addition Goodwyn's Moses and Aaron, Lib. 5, Cap. 1, and 3, and 4. 3 Ed, and Selden De Synedriis,

Maimonides in Tr. Sanhedrin, (Chap. 1 to 4 incl.,) treats at length of the mode of continuance.

The Sanhedrin existed in the days of Jesus of Nazareth, as a body having jurisdiction. The difference between Elden "Zekenim," "Presbyteroi," and Scribes, "Sophrem," "Grammateis," will be pointed out hereafter.

The Sanhedrin was the great national council. Its members were permanent, and as I have already stated, they themselves filled up any vacancy in their number. For in law the Sanhedrin never died, but was considered as the self-same body which Moses in the first instance had convened, and which had never become extinct. None but those who were called by the Sanhedrin itself, had a right to sit in that body.

There were three elders in every synagogue. They were appointed by "Semicha," which word Selden renders "per manus impositionem," but which Maimonides himself (*in loco*) goes on to explain : "They do not actually lay their hands on the head of the elder, but they address (proclaim) him as Rabbi, and announce to him : Thou art ordained, and hast authority to judge even in penal cases."

The judges so ordained were not ex-officio members of the Sanhedrin, as they were not co-ordinate but inferior ; as an order *per se* they were not represented in that body.

The great Sanhedrins, as supreme expounders of the lex scripta had legislatorial as well as judicial authority. Their enactments are styled " oral law," to distinguish them from the law of Moses.

All those who had been ordained, whether they held office as triumvirs, as assessors in the minor Sanhedrin (of 23) or in the great Sanhedrin were as a class called " Sopherim," *Grammateis*, which the English version translates literally " Scribes," but which Luther more properly renders " Schriftgelehete " Doctores Juris. It was from their body that all vacancies in judicial offices were filled up. Each of them, as a recognized teacher, claimed for his person respect, and for his opinion authority ; though of course such of them only as held public office possessed executive power.

The chief priests, even the high priest himself, were not *ex-officio* members of the Sanhedrin; though it was considered desirable, but not indispensible, that there should be priests and

Levites in that body. They could only aspire to become members if their learning qualified them, and had to obtain the Semicha, and be ordained as "Sopherim" Scribes, before they could become Elders, "Zekenim."

Respecting the number of Elders appointed in the first instance, commentators are of opinion that in order to avoid creating jealousies between the tribes, six Elders were taken from each tribe. But as the divine command positively fixed the number at 70, two were excluded by lot in manner following. Seventy tickets, with the word "Elder" inscribed on them, were put into an urn together, with two blank tickets. Each of the 72 men appointed drew a ticket; and the two who drew the blanks were excluded. Tradition relates that the two thus excluded were Eldad and Medad, (Numbers xi,) to whom, however, as a testimonial to their moral worth, the gift of prophecy was granted as well as to the 70.

With the extinction of Hasmonean royalty, and still more with the reduction of Judea by the Romans to a province of their great empire, the Sanhedrin lost much of its power and importance, though it still remained the great council of the Jews. Forty years before the destruction of Jerusalem, the Sanhedrin no longer inflicted punishment of death. Whether the power so to do was voluntarily renounced, as the Talmud relates, or whether the Romans deprived the Sanhedrin thereof, is uncertain. The presidency of the Sanhedrin became hereditary in the house of Hellel in the family of David, during four generations before the destruction, and several generations after the destruction of Jerusalem."

It is deducible, from this and other authorities, that the original institution of the Council as directed by God himself, (Numbers Ch. 11,) with the promise of his spirit, was rendered a fixed body in the Jewish Polity; that it continued, with varying extent of power and influence, for a long period; that its office was judicial, and perhaps legislative; that it was termed the seventy or Sanhedrin; and that its chief members were the Elden, Zenechin, or Presbyteroi. These facts will not be without use in illustrating the early institutions of the Christian Church.

We are to remember also, that two writers of such great eminence and learning as Grotius and Selden, sustain the position, that the Christian Church was in all its form and polity, modelled upon the Jewish.

When we begin the consideration of the system in that church, the first assembled body which strikes our attention, is the Council at Jerusalem, convened in the year 46 of the Christian era.

The judicial character of that Council has not perhaps been sufficiently attended to. It was primarily and principally a Judicial Tribunal.

It was convened to settle a single point which had become the subject of discussion and disagreement at Antioch. The consideration of the Council was called to that point, and a decision of it was made. That decision was an exposition and application of the law of the church.

The question raised and submitted was, whether the Gentile proselytes, except they were circumcised after the manner of Moses, could be saved.

Upon this question Paul and Barnabas disputed with the men of Judea, and the agreement was, to refer the question to the Apostles and Elders at Jerusalem.

The same question was raised or supported by certain of the Pharisees at Jerusalem, and to determine the point, the Council was convened. After much discussion, the views of the Apostle Peter were presented, audience was given to Barnabas and Saul; and the matter terminated with the expression of the opinion of James, which became the judgment of the Council.

This conclusion involved the strict judicial determination of the question submitted. That is contained in the clause, " We will not trouble them" (upon this point), " which, among the Gentiles are turned to God." And again, " We have heard that some who went out from us have troubled you with words saying, ye must be circumcised and keep the law, to whom we gave no such commandment."

But the Council proceeded farther, and declared that they would lay upon the converts no greater burthen than these necessary things, " that they abstain from meats offered to idols, &c."

Although this specification of what should be imposed involved the judgment that circumcision was not essential, yet it was not in strictness necessary to the judgment, nor a necessary corollary from it. These injunctions were properly Legislative ordinances for the government of the Proselytes.

And thus we find, in this first and most solemn assembly of the church, the model of the most ancient councils of which we have any reliable notice. It discharged, as they did, the functions of the highest tribunal, and exercised the highest Legislative power.

The next material enquiry is, who composed that council?

It appears from the narrative that Peter and James were there. It is argued by Dr. Hammond that this was not James, one of the twelve, but James the brother of the Lord, termed the 13th Apostle, and Bishop of Jerusalem.

The same author proves from several texts of Scripture that John was also present. (*a.*) There can be no reason to doubt that Paul and Barnabas also acted as members, with equal powers.(*b*).

The Romish writers contend, that Peter was the head of the council, resting chiefly on the fact of his speaking first. Some authors on the other side insist, that James possessed the ultimate power of decision, relying upon phrase, " My sentence is therefore, &c." It seems to me that each of these opinions is easily refuted from the narrative itself. The view of Dr. Hammond that James was the Presiding Officer, as the particular Apostle or Bishop of Jerusalem, seems the best supported.

The next class of members mentioned is the Elders.

Who these Elders were—how constituted—and the source and extent of their power is a question of great interest. Although it is not necessarily connected with the present subject, I beg to submit in a note some observations upon it. (*c.*)

The more important relative point is one which has been much controverted, viz.: whether the whole authority of the council did not vest in the Apostles and Elders alone; or whether the Brethren being Laymen, did participate in it.

It will be sufficient for the present argument to observe, that while the term Elders is sometimes used to denote seniors in age,

(*a.*) Notes on Acts 15, and on Gallatians, ch. 2, v. 1.

(*b.*) Bishop Beveridge says, (after citing Acts, cap. 15,) " In which place we read that when the controversy arose among the first Christians as to imposing circumcision and the law of Moses upon the Gentiles, Paul and Barnabas and others went up from Antioch to Jerusalem; and there, with the Apostles and Elders, held a Synod." Indeed upon the doctrine of the parity of the Apostles, Paul and Barnabas must have had seats. See Molynaeus vol. 4, p. 446. *Sur les Edits, contre les abus des Papes.*

(*c.*) Appendix Note, No. 1.

2

it is undoubtedly generally employed as denoting a class of persons.

1. And first, the reference of the question was to the Apostles and Elders, without naming any others. " They determined that Paul and Barnabas and others of them should go up to Jerusalem, *unto the Apostles and Elders*, about this question." (Acts 15, 12.)

" *The Church* brought them on their way." Doubtless this means, that the members, as they passed along, assisted them.

2. Upon their arrival at Jerusalem, they were received of the church, presumed to mean the members generally, " and of the Apostles and Elders," again contradistinguished.

3. The convocation of those to hear and decide the matter, was the Apostles and Elders solely. " And the Apostles and Elders came together to consider of this matter." (Acts 15, v. 8.)

4. The inference is a fair one, though not conclusive, that they who took part in the discussion were of the number or class of those who were convened. There had been much disputing before Peter rose up.

5. Paul and Timothy, on their subsequent journey, " as they went through the cities, delivered them the decrees to keep, *which were ordained of the Apostles and Elders*, which were at Jerusalem." (Acts 16, v. 45.)

Thus stands the argument from the record itself, of the exclusive power of the Apostles and Elders to declare the law of the church, and to enact new laws. It is impossible to deny that it possesses great force.

What is opposed to it ?

Upon the termination of the discussion by the expression of the opinion of James, it is stated, " Then it pleased the Apostles and Elders, with the whole church, to send chosen men of their own company to Antioch with Paul and Barnabas, and they wrote letters by them after this manner—"

And then the salutation of the letter is as follows : " The Apostles and Elders, and Brethren send greeting unto the Brethren which are of the Gentiles in Antioch, &c."

The letter then runs in the plural, " For as much as we have heard." " We have sent therefore."

It may be assumed, and it is a very reasonable assumption, that a considerable body of the members of the church at Jerusalem, were present at this Assembly. The supposition which is by far the most consistent with every part of the transaction is, that the Apostles and Elders made known their determination to the Disciples thus present, and that it received their approval. The letter then, as matter of form, would run in the name of all, and might be supposed to receive additional weight from being sanctioned by all. The interjectional form of the clause, " with the whole church," favors this view.

The weight of authority appears to me decidedly to support the proposition, that the actual power of the Council vested in the Apostles and Elders alone. (a.)

I have elsewhere remarked, that the seat of authority and council in the first part of the Apostolic age was at Jerusalem. From thence the Apostles went upon their missions, and thither they returned. Some of them appear to have continually resided there. (b.)

But as the number of converts increased, and age or circumstances prevented the personal visits of the apostles, the government of the church in particular regions was committed to Bishops permanently located; and the judicial, as well as other powers of government, was conferred upon them. This is shown, among other texts, by the injunction of St. Paul to Timothy, not to receive an accusation against an Elder, but at the mouth of two or three witnesses.

That the final judicial authority in his diocese resided in the Bishop, seems to me incontrovertible. I have in the note (c) shown that the quotation of Herscher, from the 4th Council of Carthage, is a mistake. It is not that a sentence was void without the consent of the Presbyters, (*sententia*) but without their presence (*presentia*).

(*a.*) See appendix, note 2, for some further observations upon this subject.

(*b.*) Barrow on the Supremacy, p. 129. " The office of an Apostle and a Bishop are not in their nature well consistent. An apostleship is an extraordinary office charged with the management and government of the whole world, and calling for an answerable care, (the apostles being rulers, as St. Chrysostom saith, ordained of God, rulers not taking several nations or cities, but all of them in common entrusted with the whole world,") but Episcopacy is an ordinary standing charge affixed to one place, and requiring a special attendance there; Bishops being Pastors who, as St. Chrysostom saith, do sit and are employed in one place."

(*c.*) No. II,

And I apprehend that all the passages in the Epistles of Cyprian, so often quoted on this topic, may be construed by the light of this canon of Carthage, although the latter was of later date. They then mean merely, that the acts of a Bishop, a Synod, or a Tribunal, were announced to all the members of the immediate church or precinct, and their approbation was obtained as matter of prudence, but nothing more. In truth there is but one clause in those passages, which is not as consistent with this meaning as with any other ; and even that clause is not irreconcilable. (a.)

The exercise of this jurisdiction of Bishops extended, by the consent of early Christian Emperors, to the amicable arbitration of civil suits of laymen ; and the jurisdiction over clerical persons was universal, except as modified by the gradual encroachment of the Popes. From the necessity of the case, and perhaps from the growth of ease and indifference, the exercise of judicial power was partly deputed to others. The Canonists attribute much evil to this delegation. (b.)

I pass over with regret the interesting subject of the mighty influence which the Ecclesiastics of England exercised in the judicial system of the kingdom. It was the necessity of the people, far more than the ambition of prelates, which gave them such extensive power. It was because they nearly engrossed the appropriate learning and ability of the age; because in their tribunals alone was justice administered with something of order and something of equity ; and because their acquaintance with the canon law brought them to a knowledge of the civil law, its sister science. Thus through clerical agency, the wise and comprehensive principles of that code were shed abroad in England, ameliorating the rigidity of the common law, and making her jurisprudence worthy a people instructed and free.

(a.) See these passages as quoted by Barow on the Supremacy, p. 244–245 notes

(b.) Incredibile dictu, quantum procedente tempore abusus jurisdictionis Ecclesiasticæ creverit. Maxime ubi Romana Curia, (amplificandæ potestatis studiosissima) incepit indies magis magisque Episcoporum jura invadere, causas quodlibet ad se evocare, et conservatores ut vocant, in Provinciis constituere. Incrementum maximum adjecit quod Episcopi contentiosam jurisdictionem officialibus committerent; de quo in sæculo 12 alté conquerebatur Petrus Blesensis, Epistola 25. (Van Espen Tractatus De Recursu ad Principem, cap. i. § 7.)

In various portions of the author's former work are notices of the judicial administration of the discipline of the church in colonial times; of the gradual changes which have been wrought, and extended details as to the existing systems in the different dioceses. To these I beg to refer. (*a.*)

The proposed canon is intended to embrace an entire system of discipline, to be established by the authority of the General Convention. Two questions must then, in the first instance, be determined. *First*, whether the power to regulate the matter exists in that convention; and *next*, whether it is expedient to exercise it, if it does exist. (*b.*)

In regard to the first question, I beg leave to refer to the observations of the author in another work. (c). The opposite views of the matter are there stated, and the author felt at the time some doubts upon the question. Further reflection has removed those doubts; and in my humble opinion, the power of the General Convention may be sustained upon the following grounds. Other reasons of greater strength may occur to abler minds.

The General Convention has become, since 1792, the national council, the pre-eminent synod of the Protestant Episcopal Church in the United States. It is that church by representation. Every power which legally and generally appertains to such a council, vests in this convention. There must be express words or necessary implication to prevent the existence of the power—not words to confer it. No authority more essentially appertains to a general council than that of prescribing and regulating the system of discipline. All precedent attests its existence. Therefore we are to enquire, whether the clause in the fifth article of the constitution, that "in every diocese the mode of trying presbyters and deacons *may* be instituted by the convention of the diocese," is a prohibition of the exercise of the power by the General Convention.

(*a.*) Introduction, p. 26- 29. Page 383, 395, &c.

(*b.*) An examination of the first two chapters of the canon will show that the provisions may very readily be adopted by a diocesan convention separately; and they may, in this respect, at any rate, be found useful.

(*c.*) Hoffman on the Laws of the Church, p. 154.

Now the language certainly admits the construction, that this is a permission only—a declaration that the several dioceses may exercise the power so long as the General Convention forbears to do so. And this construction best agrees with a general principle of law, that where a right or a power which concerns the public weal, is granted by a public authority to another, the language is to be construed strictly in favor of the grantor.

Again, it is unquestionable, that this was the construction understood and intended by the framers of the change, and by the General Convention in 1841, when it was made. Dr. Hawks states (a) that a canon was prepared in 1835 and 1838, upon the subject of discipline, and that it was considered doubtful whether a canon could be made while the constitution remained unaltered. Hence, in 1841, the word " may " was substituted for the word " shall.'

Next, upon the question of expediency. If this union of dioceses is to fulfil its purposes—if it is to keep together the members of the apostolic church throughout the land with one mind and one heart, it must supply that crying want of clergy and people, a settled course of justice. Most true it is, that in every diocese there are regulations in which some elements of a perfect system exist. These are more or less sufficient for their separate spheres: but they are not universal. What are they for a church at large—a church seeking uniformity, consistency, and strength in all her internal system of regulation, as well as in her heaven-born doctrine? Whence can these arise but from one controlling body?

But let it be carefully noticed, that while in the system suggested, a general code emanating from the paramount authority, would govern in every diocese, and lead to this uniformity and precision, the whole machinery for administering it, is almost entirely diocesan and local. Existing bodies of diocesan establishments, or bodies to be established by conventions, are the instruments to carry it into effect. The method of appealing exhibits this. Contrary to my first impression, I have made the appellate tribunal one of purely diocesan organization and power. This principle is only abandoned in the cases of proceedings for heresy or false doctrine, where it could not be to adhered to, if an appeal is at all allowed.

(a.) Constitution and Canons 34 and 57.

The proposed canon is divided into three chapters. The first re- _{Division of the Canon.} lates to the offences and trials of ministers other than bishops ; the second to courts of appeal for such trials ; and the third to the trials of bishops.(*a*)

The first chapter comprises twelve sections. The first two sections embrace a definition of terms which it is presumed will save much repetition ; and also some necessary directions as to the ecclesiastical authority to direct proceedings.

Third Section.—The *third* section (*b*) relates to the amenability of ministers. It will be perceived that a clause is added to the existing canon, (5th of 1835,) viz. : " in the manner and under the provisions hereafter contained." This will be necessary, or at least highly expedient, if the system should at all be adopted.

In a case in New York, a member of a court appointed while the standing committee was exercising its power, took the ground, that the appointment was void, because of an alleged participation of the lay members in forming the court, and approving the presentment.

An answer was given satisfactory to the committee upon the facts of the case, that the clerical members, or three at least, had united in the acts ; and that the concurrence of persons not entitled to act, would not vitiate the proceeding. But the author submitted another view. He was led to the careful examination of this canon, because if the participation of the lay members of a standing committee in the preliminary measures for forming a court, although acting under a Diocesan canon, was illegal, then the provisions in many dioceses, and particularly the matured system in Maryland, was unconstitutional. The court there is to be appointed by the Bishop, with the consent of a majority of the convention. The author became convinced that the canon meant to forbid the action of any diocese, by which the power of actually trying and judging should be committed to any but Bishops or Presbyters. The history of the institution of tribunals in colonial

---

(*a*) It is proposed to complete the system by adding a chapter on the discipline of the laity, and another to comprise various miscellaneous provisions for discipline, such as the canon respecting intrusions, differences with parishes, &c.

(*b*) The author respectfully submits an examination of the section in connection with the remarks.

and state periods, he thought led to this result; and a diocese was at liberty to vest the power of instituting a court, and making all previous arrangements, in a body consisting in part of laymen.

The last clause making the party responsible to the authority of the diocese in which he was canonically resident, wherever the offences were committed, was suggested by an exception to jurisdiction which was taken in the same case in New York above referred to. The law as it now stands appears to me clear, but the clause removes all question. The view taken in the standing committee was this.

It is a settled general rule of canon law, that *forum sequitur reum*, not *delictum*. A case in Ireland recognizes this, (*a*.) although shewing that under certain Irish canons, there were exceptions. The canon of amenability rather recognizes this rule, by providing that the clergyman is to be amenable to the authority of the diocese in which he is canonically resident at the time of the charge.

The sixth canon of 1850, seems also impliedly to admit it, by authorizing the authority of a diocese in which a minister is transiently resident, to administer discipline to a certain extent.

Although the canon originally (viz. : in 1810.) contained the words, "for any offence committed by him in any diocese," yet it is not supposed that the omission was a change of the rule. The clause probably was deemed unnecessary.

ENUMERATION OF OFFENCES.

Fourth Section.—The fourth section contains an enumeration of punishable offences.

The first subdivision is taken chiefly from the existing canon of the General Convention, and a few clauses from canons of particular dioceses.

Among the latter is one not in the general canon, viz. : Schism, or a separation from the communion of the church. In the author's former work, (p. 391,) it was sought to be shewn that in fact, schism was merely separation from the communion, and the Eng-

---

(*a*.) Office of the Judge v. Nixon, 1 Milmans' Rep. 390.

lish canons directed against the maintaining of schismatical opinions as well as schism itself, were referred to. A canonical sense then, if not the whole sense of the phrase, was separation, and this was made a ground of trial in the canon of Maryland.

I have so defined it, as far as it is to be a punishable offence ; and it is included in the first subdivision, as it is to be determined merely as a matter of fact, not of opinion, as the maintaining of schismatical doctrines would be.

The next subdivision relates to heresy and false doctrine. With respect to the former, I believe no difference of opinion exists as to the propriety of enumerating it as a punishable offence, nor perhaps of supplying some general guide or standard for defining it. But as to the teaching or inculcating false doctrine, and how to deal with the matter by express enactment, is I think the most difficult part of this whole subject.

In the True Catholic for April, 1853, the able editor has discussed the matter at length. In the late Convention of Virginia, a committee expressed disapprobation of any plan of appeals which should lead to the precise determination of what is erroneous doctrine. A judicious writer in the Church Register of June 11th, 1853, distrusts the expediency of an attempt to legislate upon the subject.

It may be considered in the first place whether the existing law of the church does not sanction a presentment for teaching false or erroneous doctrine.

Next, if it does so, whether the limits or standards of false or erroneous doctrine should be formally defined ; and if it does not, whether legislation upon the subject is expedient, and to what extent ; and lastly, what should be the instruments or mode of administering this branch of discipline.

FIRST.—In some dioceses this question is settled by particular enactment. Thus, in Connecticut, " the disseminating or countenancing opinions contrary to the doctrines of the Protestant Episcopal Church in the United States," is enumerated. In Vermont, under the 8th article of the Constitution, a presentment may be made for " error in religion, whether it respects faith or morals," and the 1st article recognizes the Book of Common Prayer, &c., as, next to the Scriptures, the rule of the church. In

Georgia, the second canon specifies error in doctrine as a triable offence.

The test of the question would fairly be, whether a presentment in such a case as that of the Reverend Mr. Prescott, could be made in the diocese of New York for example, so that it could not be dismissed on the ground of the alleged offence not being one over which jurisdiction is given.

I think it would be, and could be sustained under the 27th canon of the General Convention. I submit in the note the form of a presentment to meet such a case. (a.) I need scarcely disclaim the presumption of judging whether the opinions of the Reverend gentleman were erroneous or not.

I state another case taken from an actual trial. In England, in the year 1842, the Rev. Mr. Head was articled against for publishing the most outrageous attack upon the Prayer Book. He was proceeded against for depravation or derogation of the Book of Common Prayer, as it is termed, and was suspended. (See 3 Curteis Rep., 567.) The articles will be found in Coote's Eccles. Pr., p. 187. If we could imagine that any minister of our church could use the shocking language of Mr. Head, I conceive that as the law now stands, he could be reached. I submit the sketch of such a presentment in the note. (b.)

Again the frame of a presentment adapted to the case of Hodgson H. Oakley, (c.) will be found not only illustrative of the argument, but valuable in several particulars. And lastly, in relation to the most interesting and important case perhaps ever brought before an English Ecclesiatical tribunal, the Gosham case, I believe the very question can be legally presented for judicial decision in any diocese. (See note v.)

The perusal of the forms submitted will I think unfold the argument better than any other mode. The following, however, is an abstract of it.

A minister is liable to presentment and trial, under the 27th canon of the General Convention of 1832, for a violation of the Constitution of the Church.

Such a violation consists in doing what is forbidden therein, or omitting to do what is commanded therein.

(a.) Appendix Note III.   (c.) 1 Robertson's Eccl. Rep. p. I.   (b.) Note IV.

Conformity to the doctrine and worship of the church is enjoined by that Constitution. Not to conform thereto is to violate it.

Non-conformity consists, among other things, in holding and teaching doctrines which this church has denied or disclaimed, expressly, or by just inference from what she does hold. It consists also in holding and teaching that which this church has not received, provided the same is repugnant to that which she hath received.

And it also consists in not holding and teaching that which this church does expressly or by manifest inference, hold and require to be taught.

The standards by which such conformity or non-conformity are to be tested are—The Book of Common Prayer; the order or office entitled " The form or manner of making, ordaining, and consecrating Bishops, Priests, and Deacons; and the Articles of Religion; as the same are respectively established by the General Convention.

From all which it may be concluded that it is the doctrine of the church, that auricular confession of sins to a Priest is not allowable or warrantable at all times or places.

That it is the doctrine of this church that auricular confession of sins to a priest is not allowable or warranted at any other times or any other occasions except, &c. See the presentment note III.

The propositions are then stated in a negative form, that the alleged doctrines are not conformable to the doctrine of the church; and then the allegations of what is supposed to have been held and taught are made.

If these views are correct, the object of the third subdivision of the fourth section will be apparent. The whole scheme of proceedings in a case of heresy or false doctrine is different from that in the case of any other violation of the Constitution.

If, then, there is reason to suppose that the teaching erroneous or false doctrine may now be the subject of a presentment, the next question is, should an attempt be made to define as accurately as may be, by Legislative declarations, what are false doctrines, or rather to fix a standard for trying them. No doubt, this question is the same in practice, whether such offences are now triable, or are made so by a new enactment.

The author of the able article in the True Catholic, before noticed, does not, of course, aim at anything like an enumeration or specification. His object is to supply a standard for testing false doctrine, and also a rule for interpreting the standard.

In the Project of a canon for the trial of Bishops, afterwards noticed, this idea is placed in a definite form thus : " The teaching of the church is to be considered as contained in the Book of Common Prayer, including the articles and all offices comprised in the table of contents. No doctrine shall be adjudged contrary to the teaching of this church, which is not contrary to some passage or passages contained in that book, taken in their literal and grammatical sense. Nothing shall be adjudged the literal and grammatical sense of any part of said book, which is inconsistent with the literal and grammatical sense of any other portion thereof."

It is obvious that great pains have been taken in selecting the language used on this subject. I suggest, with hesitation, whether the rule is not laid down rather too rigidly. Take, for example, the doctrine of the Immaculate Conception, lately so boldly revived. I do not now remember a passage strictly and literally contrary to it. Probably our compilers never imagined that such a conceit was to arise again. It is not taught; and what is taught is, by just inference, repugnant to it.

Whether again, any Legislative rules of interpretation will be effectual may be open to question. The judges will exercise the right of interpreting the rule as well as the standard. The subject has been newly brought before the church in the article referred to, and deserves further and careful consideration.

For the present, I have confined the provision in the canon submitted, to the settling of the standard.

We are now brought, lastly, to the consideration of what shall be the mode of settling these questions of heresy and false doctrine. Of course, the Bishop in every diocese must be the first judge ; and as our law now stands, he is the final judge. If it be expedient that his judgment should be revised, an appellate court is essential. And the formation of an appellate court must be upon the system of associate Bishops of the vicinity or otherwise ; or upon that of the whole body of Bishops.

This most important question has not yet aroused much of the thought of the clergy. There has been little cause to consider it. I presume to predict that it will demand hereafter their most anxious deliberation.

The leading enquiry is whether the clergy will be content, that the ultimate decision, upon questions of sound or unsound doctrine, shall rest with a single Bishop. They have the precedent of the course of the church for every age, as I believe, saying, it shall not; that deposition cannot be inflicted upon them by the voice of one Bishop, unless they decline to appeal.

The system of comprovincial or associate Bishops of the vicinity has the recommendation of antiquity, of facility in discharging the duty, of prompt decisions, and of the higher confidence to be inspired by the decision of a number of Bishops unitedly deliberating upon the question. It has the evil of authoritatively settling the rule in one body of dioceses, which may be as fully settled very differently in another.

On the other side, the attempt to bring all the cases which will arise on this subject before the whole bench of Bishops, by a direct appeal to them, seems utterly impracticable.

This subject does most peculiarly belong to the clergy to determine. I only invoke their attention to it in my suggestions, as one of rising importance, to which their best wisdom will have to be directed.

The plan which I look upon, after some hesitation, as most satisfactory, is one of collegiate dioceses; the practical result of which will be, that not less than five Bishops, including the one whose decision is appealed from, must concur in a sentence for heresy or false doctrine. The concurrence of this number shall be sufficient for a sentence of suspension; but if deposition is pronounced, an appeal may be taken to the whole bench; and wherever the decision is by less than five Bishops, such appeal may always be taken.

The *Fifth Section* provides, as a substitute for the inquiry which may be directed upon public rumor, a proceeding by consent in a quiet and summary method, before two Presbyters and one Layman. This plan was suggested by a part of the Statute 4th, Victoria; but the inconvenience of that plan was, that the inquiry began before a consent to be bound was obtained, and it was only, even after the examination of witnesses, that if the accused agreed to it, a sentence might be pronounced. I observe that this system has lately been spoken of as not working favorably. In truth it enables the accused to have the advantages of a second formal trial, after what may have been a full investigation of the facts and evidence against him. Unless his consent was obtained, articles were to be filed against him, founded upon the depositions returned, and a new trial had. A canon lately submitted to the convention of Massachusetts, contains a similar principle to the provision now suggested.(a)

The standing committee of New York, in the course of some experience, were much indisposed to proceed under this clause of the canon relating to public rumor. Our New York canon, adopted under the general canon, has the words " or otherwise" added to the phrase, " by public rumor." In the cases before that committee, there was always something of a statement and written information from a reliable source, though of course not in a definite or technical form.

In truth the provision seems to rest upon an adoption of the *fama clamosa* of the canon law ; and if we look to that by the light of English authority, we shall see how strong must be the ill fame to justify a proceeding which after all is a partial trial. It was the attendant of the system of Purgation. If a person lay under a common suspicion or public fame of any vice, though there was not proof plain enough to convict him, he might be summoned befor the spiritual judge and put upon his oath, backed by the oath of five of his neighbors, that they believed him. Bishop Gibson says,(b) " whenever the life and conversation of any person hath drawn upon him such a strong and general presumption of guilt, that though he swears himself innocent, six or seven persons cannot be found in a whole parish who believe he swears true, such a one seems to be fully ripe for the shame of a public penance."(c)

(a) Canon proposed May, 1853.

(b) Codex Tit. 46, p. 1032.

(c) The statute of Charles II. abrogated the oath of purgation as far as the accused was concerned.

Again, as far as my information extends, the inquiry under the canon is *ex parte*. This is so objectionable, that every method should be tried to avoid it. The result of an inquiry, either by a body of clergymen and laymen, or of clergymen only, of standing, affixes a stigma which no thought of its *ex parte* character can efface ; and worse than this, the members of this board of inquiry, by the provisions of numerous diocese, become the presenters, unavoidably zealous to sustain their own determination. The investigation, even if it result in an acquittal, is injurious without any of the advantages of a definite trial.

And yet, if notice is given to the accused, and he attends and presents his case, the whole proceeding becomes a trial, and ought to be one and a final one, so far as the collection of the evidence is concerned ; otherwise we adopt the dangerous principle of the English statute, which has been upon experiment strongly disapproved of.

The plan suggested avoids or lessens these objections. If the accused, upon a private summons confesses the allegations, the matter is disposed of in a summary and quiet mode. If he does not confess, a tribunal of inquiry may, by his consent, be formed, and a decision obtained in a manner as free from publicity and delay as possible ; and if he will not consent, then the information on which the ecclesiastical authority has acted, is to be referred to the standing committee, who may present on that information, if sufficiently definite, or institute an inquiry. In this case only is the system of a preliminary inquiry retained, and really because I do not see how to get rid of it altogether.

CHARGE AND PRESENTMENT.

The *Sixth Section* relates to the mode of preferring a charge, and making a presentment against a minister.

Some observation will explain the object of this and numerous other provisions throughout the canon.

In the first place, I adhere to what I consider a fundamental doctrine of the church, that the ultimate judicial authority in every diocese rests in its Bishop. This seems an essential element of Diocesan Episcopacy, and I consider this principle to be recognized and embodied in the sixth article of the General Constitution of the Church. It is there provided that none but a Bishop shall pronounce sentence of admonition, suspension, or degradation from the ministry.

We cannot suppose that this means only, that the formal ceremony of declaring the sentence is left to a Bishop; that he acts only as the Doomster of the old Scottish Courts. On the contrary it is the solemn enunciation of the great principle of judicial authority and responsibility. A Bishop assumes, with his consecration vow, this most serious duty; and the sin of every wilful or heedless judgment, and the misfortune of every error lies upon him. There is nó case in which he can now be deprived of the right, or escape from the obligation, of a deliberate revision of every sentence, and its grounds in fact and law. (a)

2. But while this principle is, as I believe, observed, it has been deemed of great importance to keep a bishop from every participation in the preliminary proceedings for a trial; from any part in the details and business attending it, and from any office whatever, but that of ultimate judgment. It is, I think, obvious that these details will generally be better carried on by persons more skilled in similar matters; and it is of no little moment that he who is ultimately to review every act, should not be subject to the bias of sustaining proceedings, slight or essential, which have been performed or sanctioned by himself. From the moment then, that a case against a clergyman assumes a contentious form, the bishop in the scheme submitted, performs no office whatever but the final and supreme one.

3. It will be seen that the duty of taking or supervising all the

(a) It is in this view that I cannot but think the decision of the Bishop of Massachusetts in the last stage of the Rev. Mr. Prescott's case was erroneous. It is understood that he supposed his office was purely ministerial; that the canon had affixed the sentence necessarily which he must pronounce, without examining for himself into the validity of that sentence.

It may be first remarked that the canon of Massachusetts referred to, is not that *the Court* shall pronounce the sentence in cases of a neglect to appear for trial, but only that a sentence of suspension *shall* be pronounced. But if a canon expressly directed the Court to do so, I conceive it would be illegal and void under the constitutional provision before referred to. The similar canons of most Dioceses expressly provide, that the sentence in this case also shall be pronounced by the Bishop. Such canons are only conformable to the law; they do not make it. The direction to pronounce a sentence is necessarily subject to the right to decide whether it should be made.

preliminary steps upon a trial—the settlement of a presentment, and all the ministerial acts to conduct it to an issue, are left to the standing committees of the dioceses. I do not see in what body these offices can be better lodged. Composed, as they almost universally are, of experienced clergymen, and in every diocese but two, of a number of prominent laymen, usually some lawyers of reputation among them, the probability of a lawful and just course being pursued is at least as great as in any other mode I have heard suggested.

This system, to a very considerable extent, exists already in various dioceses. The present plan makes it incumbent on the standing committee to prepare the presentment, not merely to approve it.

4. There is another point which especially, at present, deserves consideration. It relates to the framing of a presentment, the construction of it so as to comprise a canonical offence—such offence legally and properly alleged—and the facts on which it rests set forth precisely, and with all regard to the essentials of time, place, and circumstances.

In order to secure this, it will be seen that after the allegations of an offence are received, however loosely and irregularly drawn, if they contain the necessary elements of a presentment, the standing committee is to put them in legal form. It is their duty to act in this upon their responsibility, and to give the document their deliberate sanction.

Exceptions to the presentment may, however, be taken and argued before the board of triers. These may be to the form, substance, and sufficiency in law, as well as to the jurisdiction of the board ; and they, as well as every other matter of defence, may be heard and decided by the triers. Of course they will be ultimately passed upon by the Bishop. It has occurred to me, whether it would be advisable to allow what are termed exceptive allegations to be taken to a presentment, and argued in writing before the standing committee, before the record is sent for trial. This was suggested by a case in New York, in which some members of a court thought that questions of form and jurisdiction were not before them, the ecclesiastical authority having approved of the presentment. The author suggested that no approval could have such legal effect, which was not made after a hearing,

4

or an opportunity given for hearing, of the accused party; and as the canon had not provided for this in the preliminary proceeding, it was the necessary requisition of justice that the accused should be heard before the court upon this, as well as upon other points.

The delay and the complexity and nicety of pleading which may result from the course suggested, induce the author to leave the subject to the Board of Triers, especially declaring their authority to determine such questions.

Should the present or a similar scheme meet with favor, it would be of great utility to obtain a body of precedents from the dioceses, in cases well litigated, and to vary the form as might be necessary.

CONSTITUTION OF A BOARD OF TRIERS.

Section Seventh.—The system which prevails in a very large proportion of our dioceses is one, in which the original nomination of the members of a court or board is with the Bishop; and from a considerable number so designated, the accused selects a smaller number. Thus, if the Bishop chooses, the members may be as absolutely persons of his own appointment, as if the accused had had no voice in the matter.

If a Bishop sat in person, as in ancient times, with a portion of his clergy, to try a cause, no doubt his office and influence would have great weight; but, on the other hand, he would hear the witnesses and the arguments in all their freshness, and more confidence would inevitably be placed in his decision than can be now. At present he casts himself upon the great weight due to what is similar to the verdict of a jury; and if that jury is of his own selection, distrust cannot be avoided.

A most important object is to change a system which in theory at any rate is so manifestly wrong, and which nothing but uncommon scrupulousness of a man could render endurable.

The only alternative which I have seen suggested for this objectionable system is that of a permanent court, established under the authority of each diocesan Convention.

This is the system in Maryland, and has been so since the year 1847. This is the plan submitted by the Committee on Canons, to the Convention of Massachusetts of 1853; and I understand that the same scheme was suggested in the late Convention of Mississippi, where the Committee reported strongly against the existing rule of choosing judges for each particular case, out of a body named by the Bishop.

The advantages of such a system are apparent and marked. I need not dwell upon them. The objections which have suggested themselves to me are these.

The court will inevitably be the representative of the ascendant party in the particular Convention. It is true that this evil will be immeasurably less than upon the present plan, and in the author's scheme, a court of appeals for most cases is thus constituted. It seems inadvisable, however, to have both established by the same body directly.

In the next place, the opportunity is lost of gradually diffusing among the clergy at large some general knowledge of a branch of their office and duty, which it is most expedient should be possessed by them. Every clergyman who has been a member of a court upon a contested trial, will confess, that he has reaped benefit from it, not only in positive knowledge, but in the acquisition or strengthening of a valuable habit of mind.

Once more—I have long looked upon any measure which will bring together in the active discharge of a duty, the varying members of the church, as most salutary. I am not visionary enough to suppose that ultraists are to become harmonious through this, or any other means. But as to the great mass of the clergy, the more they work together, the more will their condemnation of each other be mitigated, and the more earnest, and the more successful will be the common effort to make the church felt in the justice of her laws, and the righteousness of their administration.

With these views, I have framed a plan for a Board of Triers, upon the following leading points:

Each diocese to be divided into suitable districts, having in view the civil division into cities, wards, villages, &c., each district to have a certain number of Presbyters, not exceeding fifteen. A provision for the case of smaller dioceses is made.

This body comprises the members of the Board of Triers. Certain rules are laid down for settling the district of trial. From the list of such members, the accused and a church advocate strike off names alternately, upon the plan of a struck jury, until the number is reduced to three. These constitute the clerical members of the Board.

The accused may nominate a lay assessor, and in such case the church advocate another, and the court may also appoint a layman; which they may do whether others have been nominated or not. These laymen are to have a concurrent authority, except upon the final vote and sentence. The reasons for this portion of the plan are fully stated hereafter.

It may be that an increase of the number of Presbyters to five would be judicious; but the whole of my business experience has caused a dislike to a large number, in any body expected to do much work. With this qualification, I submit the principle of the scheme with some confidence, to the judgment of the church.

Admission of the Laity.

A marked and very extensive change of opinion has taken place among our clergy, as to admitting laymen into a share of the judicial authority. The surprise of the author has been excited at discovering, how very prevalent the sentiment has become, among many of the most conservative and enlighted clergymen, that a participation in this power would tend more fully to secure their characters and stations. The fullest admission of an unfitness of ministers for the judicial office, has been made in an article in the New York Churchman, attributed to one whose qualifications go far to refute his theory. The editor of the True Catholic, with his usual discrimination, has noticed and explained the fact. Still the question is to be solved. Will the introduction of laymen into the judicial system be a correction of the admitted evils? Will it be accompanied with any evils of its own; and how far, if at all admissible, should it extend?

When we seek into the sources of the strenuous opposition of our fathers in the faith to be judged by laymen, and compare it with the favorable regard the idea now meets with, we are struck with one great point of difference. The establishment of Courts Ecclesiastical, and the subjection to lay authority, was in the hands of the Governors under their commissions from the Crown, or of Provincial Assemblies. The ancient and deep rooted aversion of the clergy to State interference—the dislike of Erastianism, exhibited in some degree in every age of the church, roused the opposition adverted to. We know that the unfortunate statute of Henry VIII., the corner stone of the surrender of the liberties of the Church of England, has met condemnation from a large body of clergy, ever since its passage; and the omens in the skies give now some glimmer of hope of its being abolished.

This feeling was strong among the clergy of the Provinces, especially at the South. The case is now different. They have been long accustomed to meet the laity in the councils of the church; to discuss the questions of the highest importance, and to unite with them in legislation. The result has been a general belief that they would be as serviceable in the judicial, as in the legislative province.

While a constitution of Chichely embodied the general law of the church, when it prohibited married clerks or laymen from taking jurisdiction of spiritual matters, under pain of excommunication, (a) yet by a constitution of Otho, judges ignorant of the law, in a doubtful case from which prejudice may arise to either party, might, at the expense of both parties, call in the counsel of a learned assessor. (b)

From the opinion expressed by the author upon the question of the share of the laity in the councils of the early church, it will be readily seen, how utterly at variance with his views is the idea of any equality of the laity in judicial power with the clergy, in spiritual matters.

I confess I cannot see, how any one who believes in a divinely constituted order of ministers, whom we are instructed to obey as possessing the rule over us, and having the watch for our souls, can Scripturally assume the right of destroying that office. God's law does not make the laity the peers of the clergy in this matter.

There are three aspects in which the subject has been pre-

(a) Apud Burns, vol 2.   (b) John of Anthon, 72.

sented to the church. The one is, of making the lay members purely advisory, with no vote in either the final judgment, or the intermediate proceedings. The second is, to make them members of the court with as full powers in every particular as the clerical members; and the third is to give them an equal voice in every stage of the proceedings, except in the verdict and decision.

The last appears to me to be the principle best adapted to meet the exigencies of the case in our land, the ends of justice, and yet preserve the great doctrine of scriptural subordination. I have drawn every portion of the canon upon the theory of recognizing an equal power in the lay members of a tribunal down to a sentence, and leaving the ultimate decision to the clergy, by requiring a majority of such members to make a judgment.

No doubt this system is liable to the observation, that if the lay members may act with equal power upon all preliminary questions, they will be able to go very far in influencing the ultimate decision. But we are to remember, that it is upon questions of the legal frame of the presentment, of jurisdiction, of the construction of the law, of the rejection or admission of evidence, that the utility of any legal assessors is to be felt.

Neither uniformity nor accuracy of decision is to be expected—if their opinions may be absolutely rejected—if they are nothing more than suggestions and advice. When the cause has been legally sifted and presented, the decision should be left to the judgment and decision of the clerical members alone. In this respect, a part of the principle which gives the control of legal questions at a trial to a judge, is discernible. A judge's office is to say to a jury what they have to determine, and what is the evidence upon which they are to determine. The decision, then, rests with them; but while the office of the judge in such a case is exclusive, that of the laymen in the present proposal is merely concurrent. To this extent, it seems to me, it ought to reach, though not further.

I have heard it remarked, and by a clergyman who was for giving a concurrent power to the lay members in every particular, that the ultimate determination still resting in a Bishop, the lay vote would not in truth decide the case. But it must be remembered, that in almost every diocese, although a clergyman cannot be degraded or suspended without the Bishop, yet the Bishop cannot find him guilty without the intervention of a court. Therefore the verdict is equally essential, and comes from an independent body. Nor is it probable that this principle will ever be relinquished.

But here it is to be carefully noticed, that the scheme confers a lay authority to this extent, only in that class of offences which does not embrace heresy or a deviation from the doctrines of the church. In the latter case a layman has no other office than a mere adviser.

An Appellate Tribunal.

Chapter 2 of the canon relates to this subject.

The necessity or importance of an Appellate Tribunal in our system has been felt by many experienced and able churchmen, and has of late assumed the form of a distinct proposition. Bishop Hopkins, as chairman of the committee on canons, in the General Convention of 1847, made a report, and presented a canon, many provisions of which were to organize such a court. And in the Convention of 1850, Mr. Wharton, of Pennsylvania, submitted a canon for consideration, which will be found in the Appendix to the Journal of 1850, p. 227, and is hereafter particularly stated.

The subject is of the greatest importance, and deserves attentive consideration. A right of appeal, of one appeal at least, has been treated as of such inherent natural justice as to have its origin in the law of nations. (a.) It has accompanied every system of jurisprudence which has emerged from barbarism, and I believe that there cannot be found a period in the history of the church, since the days of the Apostles, in which such a right has not been recognized and regulated. A reference to its prevalence, and the forms in which, at different periods it existed, may be found useful.

While, in the early ages of the church, the sentence of a bishop of a diocese was treated as of force in every other diocese, a method of redress was still open. This was provided for in the sixth canon of the Council of Nice, (A.D. 323,) permitting an enquiry to be made before the provincial synods. No intermediate appeals

(a.) Burns, vol. i. p. 57.

were known at this period. The appeal from a bishop to an Archbishop, thence to the Primate, and ultimately to the Pope, arose in the ninth century, after the promulgation of the false decretals.

The Canonists trace the progress of this papal usurpation, from appeals in causes of great moment and of a particular character, to matters of inferior importance; from definitive sentences to interlocutory judgments; and lastly, to the evocation of causes in the first instance, to the court of Rome. (a.)

The 4th canon of Antioch (A. D. 341) recognized the deposition of a Bishop by a Synod; and of a presbyter or deacon, by his own Bishop. That of Nice had provided for an appeal from the decision of a Bishop to a Synod.

The 12th canon of the Sixth Council of Carthage provided, that when a Bishop was guilty of a crime, and a greater number could not be collected, his case should be heard by twelve Bishops; a presbyter's offence by six Bishops with his own; and a deacon's by three with his own.

The commentator *Zonaras* states, that this was resorted to, in order to meet the inconveniences and delay of judgment attending an appeal to a Synod. The canon was to regulate such an appeal, not to interfere with the original Episcopal jurisdiction.

The sixth canon of the Second Council of Spain declared, that a Bishop might singly confer (ministerial) honor on a minister, but could not by his sole authority take it away. This I presume means, that he could not do so ultimately, if his decision was appealed from. Corpus Canonici, Pars. 2, p. 260.

It would be inconsistent with the whole doctrine of Episcopal authority to suppose that, in the first instance at least, the decision upon the offence of a clergyman did not rest with his Bishop, and one of the canons of a Council of Carthage proves the contrary. By the third of the third Council it is declared, after providing for the cases of Bishops, "that of the causes of other clerics, let the Bishop take cognizance singly."

The whole of these canons of Carthage deserve an accurate collation and examination, particularly the 2nd of the 1st Council;

(a.) Fleury, part 3, Inst. Can., cap. 33. *Dupin Manuel du Droit Ecclesiastique Des Appels comme d'Abus.* Van Espen de Appellationibus. Among other things an appeal to the pope, *omisso Medio*, was allowed.

the 4th of the 2nd ; the 8th of the 3d ; the 23d of the 4th ; and the 12th of the 6th Council.' (a.)

I have before adverted to the long and severe struggle between the Popes and the Sovereigns of Europe, to establish for the former an entire supremacy in the administration of justice, by way of appeal. The doctrine of the Gallican Church was, that the right of enforcing spiritual sentences was in the civil power, and that the right to see whether such sentences were just before its authority was lent to their execution, followed of course. The appeal to the Pope was rejected. (b.)

I have also traced to some extent the history of that contest in England, citing the impressive statute of Richard II, denouncing, among other papal usurpations, this right of appeal. The statute of 24th Henry VIII, cap. 12, was noticed, leaving the ultimate appeal to the Archbishops. It was also shown that the fatal statute of 25th Henry VIII, wrung from the clergy by a mingled feeling of detestation of Rome, and dread of a despot, stands as the basis of that deplorable Erastianism which diminishes the lustre of our noble mother, the true defender of the faith of the saints, the pure and majestic English Church. (c.)

In one branch of that unfortunate exhibition of the evil principle of allowing secular tribunals to judge of holy things, the Gorham case, the Court of Exchequer asserted, that the constitutions of Clarendon sanctioned an appeal to the king ; and in the House of Lords, this proposition was repeated by one of the ministers.

(a.) Apud Gratian corpus jur., canon ; 359. *Mansis. Concilia*, vol. 1. Van Espen De Appellationibus passim.

(b.) D'Hericourt Les Lois Ecclesiastiques, ch. 25, Dupin Manuel du Droit, &c., p. 243.

(c.) Since the above was written I have seen the pastoral letter of the Bishop of Exeter, of 1852. He strongly argues that the clause in the act of 25th Henry VIII, giving the appeal to the king in chancery, was but a temporary provision until the commissioners appointed under the same act should report the revision, which subsequently was known as *Reformatio Legum*, though never acted upon. The clause as to appeals in that work was, from Archdeacons and others below the rank of Bishops having jurisdiction, to the Bishop ; from Bishops to the Archbishops ; from the Archbishop to our Majesty, to be determined, if *it was a case of a grave nature, by a provincial Council, or by three or four Bishops to be appointed by us.*

Never was there a more absolute refutation of a statement than this met with from one of the bishops. He quoted the original of the constitutions, and added, "Thus it appears from the most authentic texts of the constitutions of Clarendon, that the ancient law of the land, as settled by these constitutions, is not what the recent judgment of the Court of Exchequer declares it to be. It does not give to the king the right to decide on appeal in all ecclesiastical causes; but on the contrary declares that right and duty to belong to the court of the Archbishop, forbidding the cause to be carried to the Pope. The result is, that by the ancient law of England, in accordance with sound church principles, the final decision of causes spiritual belonged to the spiritual, and not to the temporal courts, although the crown had, as it still has, a right to rule all estates of the realm, be they ecclesiastical or civil; to see and require that they all do their several duties, and to refuse to acknowledge any outward co-active power, which proceeds not from, or is not sanctioned by itself."

The system of appeals in England under the acts of 24 and 25 Henry VIII, cap. 12 and cap 19, is fully stated by Mr. Burns, (vol. 1, p. 59, &c.) The statute 1 and 2 Victoria, cap 106, regulated appeals from the Bishop to the Archbishop, and thence to the Judicial Committee of the Privy Council.

It is the exercise of that ultimate power in cases of doctrine by the Privy Council, which has awakened such earnest struggles in the church of England to reform this system. " The law of the land has, by a most unhappy mistake, intrusted to a body of men, of high character and attainments, but wholly deficient in that knowledge—the knowledge of the laws and doctrines of the church—which alone could make any person competent to the discharge of judicial duties in such a cause—the decision of a question purely spiritual, nay, strictly and undeniably doctrinal." (a.)

The subject, as before observed, has been brought before the church by propositions of the Bishop of Vermont, and of a distinguished jurist of Pennsylvania. It has been largely discussed in the church journals; and the editor of the *True Catholic* has devoted one of his able and analytical articles to its consideration. (b)

(a.) Bishop of Exeter.   (b) True Catholic, August, 1852.

A doubt is expressed in this article whether the General Convention could establish a Court of Appeal to revise the decisions of Diocesan Tribunals. The principles advocated in the author's former work, and hereinbefore stated, would sustain the power. The institution of a Court of Appeal is of course a branch of the power to establish a mode of trial. If the General Convention has that power inherently, (as it appears very clear to the author it has,) and the article of the constitution is declaratory only of the power of the dioceses until that Convention acts, then the power may be exercised in whole or in part; and especially may it be exercised, when the Diocesan Convention has not legislated upon that branch of the subject at all; and yet more clearly when, as in forming a Court of Bishops, it could not possess any authority to legislate upon the subject.

The first material point to be noticed in the proposed canon of Mr. Wharton is, that the appeal can only be taken where the case involves matter of law, and that within the jurisdiction of the general convention. The next is, that the appellate tribunal is composed of the three senior Bishops of the church after the presiding Bishop, in an order of rotation, and of three lay members of the profession of the law selected in the manner prescribed. Again, the Bishop who has made the decision appealed from, is precluded from sitting in the court.

If the case involves matter of doctrine, a majority of the Bishops forming the court must concur in the judgment. A majority of the court, all the members being duly summoned, shall constitute a quorum, and shall have authority to decide the appeal, subject to the qualification as to the concurrence of a majority of the Bishops, in matter of doctrine.

A plan of Bishop Hopkins was first presented in 1847. It involved a right of appeal from every decision of a Bishop. The presiding Bishop was to select seven Bishops at his discretion to form the Court of Appeal. The Bishop from whose judgment the appeal is taken has a right to sit, but not to take part in the decision. If the Court of Appeal be unanimous, the judgment shall be final. If not so, a further appeal may be taken to the whole college of Bishops.

On this appeal, the Bishops who have heard the first appeal have an equal voice in the judgment, and the determination of majority is conclusive.

This plan was afterwards, viz., in 1850, materially varied by the eminent Prelate. The proposed canon will be found in the Journal of 1850, p. 145. On an appeal, the appellant must add his declaration in writing that he truly believes the decision to be contrary to the laws of the church, or to the principles of justice and equity; in which declaration not less than three Presbyters, if the appellant is a Presbyter, or three laymen, if he is a layman, shall unite.

The dioceses and missionary territories shall be divided into districts, each district containing no less than three, nor more than seven Bishops, according to the direction of the House of Bishops.

A majority of the Bishops of the district shall form the court to hear the case. But an appeal may be taken from the judgment to the Bishops in council at the next General Convention. These are the leading features of the plan.

It is a source of gratification to the present writer, that the subject of an appellate tribunal having occupied his thoughts before 1850, he had sketched an outline of a scheme upon the same principle of collegiate dioceses. He then made it to have jurisdiction of all cases, by way of appeal. Subsequent reflection has led to a modification of this plan, and to restrict the office of such a court to appeals in cases of heresy and false doctrine.

The outline of the scheme now submitted is this:

A diocesan court for hearing and appeal in every case, except for heresy and false doctrine, is to be established by each diocesan convention. The section directs that seven Presbyters, and seven laymen, lawyers, shall be nominated by the convention, to form a class of members for the court. A provision is inserted to meet the case of small dioceses. The principle of striking a jury is here also introduced, though, necessarily, to a limited extent. It will be sufficient to meet the instances of personal opposition or favor. The number is to be reduced to three of each order. The judgment of this court upon all these offences shall be final.

It may be useful to state the operation of the whole scheme of trial in a small diocese. I believe the lowest number of clergymen in any diocese except Florida is thirteen. This would admit of but seven Presbyters, as members for a Board of Triers, if six were named for the Appellate Court. If four were named, nine would be left to form the members of one district of Triers. If the number of the Presbyters should be twenty, there might be two districts of eight members each.

But in cases of heresy and false doctrine, the principle of the system of Bishop Hopkins seems to me the best and most practical. Some variations have occurred to me as expedient. I have suggested the allotment of the dioceses to be made by the convention. The Bishop leaves that to the House of Bishops. The present plan provides for eight Bishops in each collegiate diocese, with one necessary variation. The Bishop allows three, and a majority to hear and decide. The Bishop admits an appeal in every case to the body of Bishops. The present plan, besides committing finally to the diocesan Appellate Court all cases, except for heresy and erroneous doctrines, proposes to give an appeal to the whole body of Bishops, even in these excepted cases, only where less than five Bishops of the collegiate diocese have concurred in a judgment.

The foregoing observations, with occasional remarks in notes upon some provisions, will explain the canon now submitted, so far as the trial of a minister, other than a Bishop, is concerned. A brief summary of the leading points will enable the reader to see whether protection is not fully secured to the clergy, and vindication for the church.

In the first place, the plan of an investigation by consent, will, it is hoped, secure a quiet and summary method of disposing of many cases.

In the next place, when open litigation takes place, a considerable body of clergymen, almost unavoidably comprising some of differing views in the church, form the class from which the Board of Triers is to be taken. The principle of a struck jury is then resorted to ; and those personally hostile or favorable, and those of extreme views, if it is judged expedient in the case, may be excluded. Then each party may choose a lay assessor, and the court another ; a provision of Mr. Wharton's canon as to the trial of Bishops, which, particularly with the power of choice given to the court, appears to me judicious.

This plan, I submit, can scarcely fail to secure a sifting, full examination of the case, and the success of the truth.

An appellate court is then established, formed of seven Presbyters and seven laymen, or less, where the small number of ministers in a diocese requires it. To this, also, the principle of a struck jury is applied. But all these provisions relate to one class of cases—a class in which the nature of the offence, and the nature of the testimony, is different from the other.

The trial of a minister for heresy or false doctrine is made to rest upon a formal presentment by Presbyters; a Court of Presbyters is to be constituted by consent, or in the manner the Presbyters are selected from the Class of Triers in the other cases. A lay adviser may be chosen by the Court to act with them, without any voice upon any question. The decision of the Bishop may be carried to a Court of Bishops, and if four of such Bishops concur with the Bishop pronouncing the sentence, the decision shall be final, except where the sentence is deposition, when an appeal will always lie to the whole body of Bishops, as well as where less than five in all have united in the judgment.

TRIAL OF A BISHOP.—CHAPTER III.

The history of the Legislation of the Church upon the subject of a trial of a Bishop, is so fully stated in the *True Catholic*, (a) that the author gladly avails himself of it. It will be seen that considerable fluctuation in a material principle has been exhibited.

The Canon of 1841, and that of 1844, vests the power of presentment in the Diocesan Convention, and in three Bishops. The proposed canon of 1847 and of 1850, takes away the power to present from the Bishops, except in the case of heresy, or doctrinal error; vesting the authority in such cases in a single Bishop. In other cases, the power is left exclusively to the Convention. Thus, with the exception noticed, the church at large would have no organ to represent it in proceeding against a Bishop.

The serious questions are whether this is right in principle, and whether it will not form a strong practical difficulty in procuring the adoption of the canon. Certainly the organ selected in the canons of 1841 and 1844 to act for the church at large, is so

(a) February, 1853.

objectionable in theory, and so deplorable in its operation, that I believe it is almost unanimously condemned.

That the selection of three Bishops to examine charges should be left to accusers, possibly bitter enemies—that they should be empowered to hear *ex parte* allegations—that they should be justified in personally searching out evidence on which to proceed—that they should be the Presenters to attend and conduct a trial, with all the weight of their character and stations, is absolutely shocking to the moral sense. No language can be too strong to condemn it.

The eminent framers of the proposed canon of 1850 swept away this office from the Bishops entirely, and left the Conventions to exercise it exclusively, except in cases of heresy and false doctrine.

Within the last month a project of a canon for the trial of Bishops has been issued, the authorship of which the readers of the *True Catholic* will trace to a very eminent source.

In this project the right of presentment is primarily placed in the Conventions in every case, except for heresy, schism, or false doctrines. But this right is not exclusive, where the charge involves crime or immorality, or a violation of the constitution and canons of the General Convention. In these instances, the decision of the Convention against a presentment is not final, but application may be made upon the same charges for an enquiry by the three Junior Bishops entitled to a seat in the House of Bishops.

The project therefore recognizes, as to this extensive and important class of cases, the demand of the church at large to be represented by an organ of its own, in examining accusations against a Bishop. My own observation leads me to conclude, that no plan which entirely rejects this principle in such cases, will be acceptable to the church.

Apart from this objection to the scheme of the canon of 1850, other objections exist against the vesting this power in a Diocesan Convention, of no trivial nature.

Upon the Project of a canon, two observations occur as deserving consideration. In the first place, it is attended with the evil and delay of a new trial for the same offence. As notice is to be given to the accusers and accused, it is obvious that the contest will be strong and earnest before the committee and the Convention. It is then to be renewed before three Bishops. The former testimony may be retaken—the former, and new witnesses produced. (a)

In the next place, there does appear to be a radical objection to clothing a legislative body, numerous, swayed by momentary impulses, and urgent to finish their labors, with what after all is a portion of judicial power. The separation of legislative from judicial offices and duties is a fundamental principle of political science. It is founded upon the deepest reasoning, and the soundest lessons of experience.

Next. Any plan which admits of Bishops being presenters in any case (except the single one of heresy and erroneous doctrine) is to my mind so objectionable, that not even the very wise and guarded provisions of the project can reconcile me to it. (See section 16.)

In the plan submitted, the Convention, so far from having the prominent place in this proceeding, can only act in special cases strictly defined—only when the dismissal of a charge by the Board of Enquirers has been by a bare majority; and then under the wise restrictions contained in the Project, and some additional check s.

In establishing a Board of Enquiry, I have made use of the standing committees in the Collegiate Dioceses respectively, those dioceses established for an Appellate Tribunal in matters of heresy and false doctrine. These committees are to designate a presbyter and layman of their number to form the class out of which the Board is to be constituted. (b) The principle of a struck jury is here also applied. Thus, if the number of dioceses, as proposed, is eight, there will be eight of each order on the list, and by striking off alternately, the body will be reduced to three of each order. I apprehend this number is large enough.

The primary power to investigate and present is thus vested; and a dismissal of the charge is made conclusive, except in certain particular cases. In these the matter may be brought before the

---

(a) Such under the 13th section would be the case; but as matter of detail it is easy of correction if desirable.

(b) A special provision is made for cases where there are no lay members of such committee.

Diocesan Convention, but under such restrictions as will rather make it a rehearing or revision, than a new investigation.

The plan now submitted in relation to a presentment for heresy or false doctrine, is the same as that of the proposed canon of 1850, and of the Project.

COURT.—The court for the trial is constituted under the canon of 1850, by drawing from a box the names of eighteen out of all the Bishops of the church, from which list the accused Bishop shall strike nine. The remaider form the court. Seven of these may form a quorum.

The Project varies, in substituting sixteen for the number, to be drawn, and allowing the accused to strike off seven. The latter, however, contains a provision as to lay assessors, which the former does not. Section nineteen declares, that every court constituted under the last section, except where the trial is for heresy or false doctrine, shall, by a majority of votes, appoint one or more communicants of the church, of the profession of the law, to be assessors, but without a vote in any case.

The objection which has occurred to me, as to the principle of these provisions, is, that it will leave the selection of a court almost entirely in the hands of the accused. Eighteen or sixteen Bishops, drawn from something like double the number, will probably, as has been observed, represent the differing views of the Bishops proportionately.(a) Then the permission to strike off seven names must generally make a court of members the most favorable to the Bishop accused. Why should the church in this selection be without a representative or a voice? I have submitted, in the plan now offered, a provision for the accused and accusers alternately striking off names from the class, until the number is reduced to nine.

With respect to the mode of forming that class, I retain the section as sometime ago it was prepared, making the Bishops in two of the dioceses, as they are numbered, the body of members for the trial of a bishop residing within any diocese thereof. It will be observed the dioceses are before arranged into four Collegiate Dioceses. The classes consist, one of the Bishops in the first and second, the other, of those in the third and fourth of such Collegiate Dioceses. I present it in this form for consideration,

(a) True Catholic Ap., 1853.

6

being doubtful, after greater reflection, whether the scheme of the canon of 1850, and the Project, may not be preferable —that is, of forming the class by lot out of the whole number of Bishops.

I propose to place lay assessors in this case upon the same footfng as in that of a minister, with a voice upon all questions, except the final judgment.

The right of appeal is also somewhat restricted. If the vote against the accused is by six Bishops, it shall be final. If less, an appeal to the whole bench may be taken, as well as where the sentence is deposition.

In cases of heresy and false doctrine, the plan provides for the trial being had before the whole bench of Bishops, without any intermediate tribunal. Generally there will be little testimony to be collected in these cases; but, when it is necessary, it is provided that a commissary may be appointed to collect it.

I submit the proposed canon to the reflection of churchmen, with as strong a sense of its imperfections as any one can feel; but with an earnest hope that its errors may be corrected, its deficiencies supplied, and what is useful in it may be matured, to the advantage and honor of the church.

CANON

OF THE PENAL LAW OF THE CHURCH.

GENERAL PROVISIONS.

SECTION I.

Definition of Terms.

Unless it shall otherwise appear from the context, the following terms, when used in this canon, shall be construed to mean as follows :

The term Ecclesiastical Authority to mean—

1. The Bishop of the Diocese in which the proceedings are had. Or,

2. An Assistant Bishop, if vested with power in the matter by his Diocesan, or with full authority by a convention under canon 6 of the General Convention of 1832, or under any other or future canon to the same effect. Or,

3. The Bishop, Assistant Bishop, or Missionary Bishop, placed in full charge of a diocese under the 4th canon of 1847, or under any other or future canon to the same effect. Or,

4. A Provisional Bishop, elected under the third canon of the General Convention of 1850, or under any other canon to the same effect. Or,

5. The Bishop of some other diocese, as is provided in Section II, hereof.

The term " Ecclesiastical Laws," shall be construed to mean all constitutions, canons, resolutions, subscriptions, engagements, vows, and laws, which now are or shall hereafter become binding upon the Bishop or minister of this church, who, or whose conduct may be brought in question under this canon; and the term " ecclesiastical offence," shall be construed to mean the violation or neglect of any one or more of such " ecclesiastical laws ;" and the word "diocese" shall be construed to mean the diocese to which such Bishop or minister as is last above mentioned shall canonically belong; and the term "minister" shall be construed to mean a deacon or presbyter only.

Whenever words importing the plural number are used, in describing or referring to any matters, parties or persons, any single matter, party or person shall be deemed to be included, although distributive words may not be used.

SECTION II.

Further Provision as to the Ecclesiastical Authority.

Subdi-
vision. 1. In case there shall be no Bishop of the diocese, or the Bishop shall be under a disability by reason of a judicial sentence, and no Provisional Bishop has been elected, or any Bishop placed in charge of the diocese, or in case the Bishop, or Assistant Bishop, or Provisional Bishop is implicated in the offence, or is related to the party called in question, within the fourth degree of the computation of the civil law, the standing committee of the diocese shall request the Bishop of some other diocese to act in the matter; and thereupon such Bishop shall be, for such particular case, the ecclesiastical authority.

2. The States and Territories under the charge of any Missionary Bishop within the United States, shall, for the purposes of this canon, as far as the same can be applied, be considered as one diocese.

Each Missionary Bishop shall have power to appoint two or more presbyters, and two or more laymen within such diocese, who shall, for the purposes of this canon, be deemed the standing committee thereof; and who may choose a president and secretary from among their number. Such Missionary Bishop shall be the ecclesiastical authority in such missionary diocese.

SECTION III.

Limitation of Proceedings.

1. No proceeding shall be instituted against a Bishop or minister for any ecclesiastical offence, unless the same be commenced within five years after the commission of the offence in question.

But when proceedings are brought in respect of an offence for which a conviction has been obtained in a civil tribunal, the suit may be commenced against the person so convicted, within five years from the date of such conviction.(*a*)

CHAPTER I.

TRIAL OF A MINISTER.

SECTION I.

Amenability of Ministers.

1. Every minister of the church shall be amenable for any ecclesiastical offence to the ecclesiastical authority of the diocese, in the manner, and under the provisions in this chapter and the next chapter contained. A minister is responsible to the authority of the Diocese to which he canonically belongs, wheresoever the offence may have been committed. (*b*)

SECTION II.

Punishable Offences. (*c*)

A minister shall be liable to inquiry, to presentment, and trial for the following ecclesiastical offences :— Subdivision. 1

For any crime or immorality, for drunkenness, profane swearing, disorderly conduct, frequenting places most liable to be abused to licentiousness ; for a violation of the constitution or canons of the church, or of the diocese to which he belongs ; for the discontinu-

---

(*a*) English Statute I Victoria, canon of Mr. Wharton, 1849. Project of a canon for the trial of a Bishop.—*True Catholic*, July, 1853.

(*b*) See remarks, ante, page 15.　　　　(*c*) See remarks, ante, page 16.

ing all exercise of the ministerial office without lawful cause; for the habitual disuse of public worship, or of the holy Eucharist according to the offices of the church; and for schism or the separating himself from the communion of the church. (*a*)

2   And also for heresy, or teaching, or maintaining heretical doctrines; or for teaching or inculcating doctrines contrary to those of this church; such teaching or maintaining being by way of writing, or printing, or preaching, or public teaching. (*b*)

3   The offences enumerated in the next preceding subdivision shall not be construed to be offences, within the first subdivision of this section, so as to warrant a proceeding for the same or any of them, in the manner provided hereafter, for proceeding under such first subdivision. (*c*)

4   Schism for the purposes of this canon, shall be understood to mean a separation from the communion of the church, with or without a union with any church or brotherhood not in communion with this church; or a declaration in writing that he the minister is no longer in communion with this church, signed by such minister.

5   Heresy, for the purposes of this canon, shall be understood to mean the openly holding and teaching any doctrine inconsistent with the Nicene Creed as contained in the Book of Common Prayer established by the General Convention of this church, and which has been adjudged and determined to be heresy by the first four General Councils of the church, or either of them.

6   The doctrine of this church is to be considered as contained in the Book of Common Prayer, including the Articles, and all the offices contained in the table of contents.

SECTION III.

Proceedings upon Consent. (*d*)

Subdivison.
1   If there is reason for supposing from public rumor, or otherwise, that a minister has been guilty of any ecclesiastical offence

(*a*) The clauses of the first subdivision except the last sentence are all take fromn the 1 and 2 sections of the 27th Canon of 1832. The last sentence is found in substance in the 5th Canon of Maryland, and in those of several other dioceses.

(*b*) See remarks ante page 16, *et seq.*   (*c*) See remarks ante page 17.

(*d*) See remarks ante page 19.

enumerated in the first subdivision of the second section hereof, the ecclesiastical authority may summon the party to appear in private ; and upon confession of the offence alleged, may pronounce such sentence as shall be proper.

In such case the accusation shall be reduced to a definite form. There shall be added thereto the confession signed by the party ; and the same, with the sentence pronounced, shall be transmitted to the secretary of the Standing Committee, to be recorded in like manner as other sentences are hereinafter directed to be recorded.

If in such case, the accused party shall not confess the 2 offence alleged, the ecclesiastical authority may, by and with his consent, appoint two presbyters and one layman to make inquiry into the truth of the accusations, and to report the facts, with their opinion thereon, as well as the evidence taken. Such presbyters and laymen may be selected in any manner which the ecclesiastical authority and the accused may agree upon.

In such case the accusation shall be reduced to form in writing. The same may if necessary be referred to any three members of the Standing Committee to settle—a general denial may be entered and annexed ; and the same shall be signed by the ecclesiastical authority and the accused.

Thereupon a commission may issue under the hand of the 3 ecclesiastical authority, to the presbyters and laymen designated, authorizing them to inquire into the truth of the matter alleged.

The record, with the commission annexed, shall forthwith be sent to the eldest of the presbyters named, who shall be the president of such Board of Enquiry.

Upon the return of the record, with the opinion of the Board, or of a majority, the ecclesiastical authority may affirm, disallow, or reverse the same, as shall appear just ; and may dismiss the accusation, or pronounce such sentence as shall be proper.

The record, with the sentence pronounced, shall thereupon be transmitted to the secretary of the Standing Committee, to be recorded, as is hereafter provided in respect to trial records, and sentences.

The ecclesiastical authority of each diocese, by and with the 4 advice of the Standing Committee, shall have power to make from time to time such orders and regulations as may be deemed proper, for the formation and continuance of such Board, its mode of proceeding and other matters, for the better carrying out the provisions of the section, provided that the same be not inconsistent herewith, or with the constitution or canons of this church.

5   If the party refuses or neglects to attend when summoned as hereinbefore mentioned, the ecclesiastical authority shall lay before the Standing Committee the information, to be acted upon as provided for hereafter.

SECTION IV.

Charge against, and Presentment of a minister.

Subdivision. A charge may be preferred against any minister of the church,

1 for any ecclesiastical offence comprised within the first subdivision
Charge of the second section of this chapter, in the manner, and under the provisions following :

2   It may be made by any three presbyters of the diocese ; or by
By whom made. any five of the wardens and vestrymen of the parish or church of which the accused is a minister, or by any five of the male communicants of such church or parish.

When the accused party is not connected with any church or parish, the charge may be made by any three presbyters of the diocese, or by any five communicants of the same.

3   The charge shall be in writing, signed by the parties making it,
Form of and shall specify the offence or offences with reasonable certainty as to the time, place and circumstances. There shall be annexed to it the names and residences of the material witnesses, and a copy of any documentary evidence relied upon.

It may be in the following form, " To the ecclesiastical autho-
" rity of the diocese of

" The subscribers, (titles and additions,) allege and charge,
" that the Rev. A. B., a minister of this church of the order of
"   (and Rector of the church or parish of
"   ,) has been guilty of certain ecclesiastical offences,
" for which he is subject to trial and censure, viz., of, &c."

" To establish which allegations and charge we refer to the affi-
" davits, certificates, documents, and to the witnesses whose
" names and places of residence are hereto annexed.

" Which charge we know to be true in substance, (or,) which
" charges, on information satisfactory to us, we believe to be
true."

If upon receiving such charge, the standing committee shall de- 4
termine that there is sufficient ground for proceeding against the
accused party, they shall make a presentment to the ecclesiastical
authority.

If they find that the charge involves a triable ecclesiastical offence, but that the same is not set forth properly as to the facts or
circumstances, they may direct the same to be added to or
amended.

When the ecclesiastical authority shall have transmitted to the 5
standing committee the information by rumor or otherwise, mentioned in the fifth section of this chapter, such committee may
proceed as follows :

If the same is sufficient in substance and particulars to frame a
presentment thereupon, a presentment may be made ; *or* such committee may institute an enquiry as to whether there is prima facie
ground for a presentment upon the allegations.

Such enquiry may be conducted according to such general regulations, as the ecclesiastical authority, by and with the advice and
consent of the standing committee, shall prescribe ; such regulations
to be reported to the ensuing Diocesan Convention for its approval,
and if approved, shall be reported by the ecclesiastical authority
to the next ensuing General Convention, for any action thereon
which may be deemed proper.

The presentment shall set forth the offence alleged, with reason- 6
able certainty as to time, place, and circumstances.

It shall be addressed to the ecclesiastical authority of the diocese, and shall be signed by all the members concurring in the
same. At least two members of each order, or four clerical members must so concur.

The standing committee shall, at the time of making such pre- 7
sentment, nominate a Church Advocate to appear on behalf of the
prosecution, which advocate shall be a presbyter belonging to the
diocese, or a layman who has been a member of some church of

7

the same for at least two years before such nomination. The nomination shall be endorsed on such presentment.

8   If upon receiving the charge hereinbefore mentioned, the standing committee shall refuse to make any presentment upon the same, the parties preferring such charge may appeal to the ecclesiastical authority from such decision ; and if the same is reversed, a church advocate shall be appointed by such authority, who shall draw up such presentment, and the subsequent proceedings shall be had as if the standing committee had made a presentment.

Such presentment shall be transmitted to the Secretary of the standing committee.

9   A copy of such presentment, certified by such Secretary, shall for all purposes be as available as the original if produced.

SECTION V.

Board of Triers.

Subdi-
vision
1   For the purpose of constituting a Board of Triers, it shall be the duty of the Ecclesiastical Authority, by and with the advice and consent of the standing committee, from time to time, to divide each diocese into districts, so that the number of Presbyters in each district shall not be less than seven, nor more than fifteen.

Provided that in any diocese where the number of Presbyters shall not exceed fifteen, the division may be made in such proportions as shall be deemed expedient, or may be omitted altogether. In the latter case the diocese shall be deemed the district. The division into districts shall be made, as near as may be, with reference to the cities, or wards of cities, villages, towns, boroughs, or counties.

The Presbyters chosen by the Convention to be members of the Diocesan Appellate Court, established under the second section of chapter two of this canon, shall not be included in the list of Presbyters in such district.

The Secretary of the standing committee shall keep a record of the division aforesaid, and of any changes made from time to time therein.

The Presbyters in such districts respectively shall be the members of the Board of Triers for the same.

When a Presentment has been prepared, the Secretary of the standing committee shall transmit to the Church Advocate a certified copy of the same, with a list of the members of the board for the district of trial ; which district shall be determined as follows :— 2

If the accused is a settled minister in charge of a parish, or cure, or an assistant minister, the district shall be that in which the church, chapel, or place of public worship in which he statedly officiates, is situated.

If the accused has no such settled charge, the district shall be that in which he resides.

And if he is absent from the diocese, the standing committee shall designate the district by lot.

The Church Advocate shall thereupon transmit a copy of the Presentment, with his nomination endorsed, and also a list of the members of such district, to the accused party ; and at the same time shall give him notice to attend before the President and Secretary of the standing committee, at a time and place to be fixed by such President ; and thereupon the party accused shall first strike from such list one of the names, and the Church Advocate shall strike off another, and so alternately, until the number shall be reduced to *three*. 3

If the accused shall neglect to attend in person, or by an agent, the President and Secretary of such committee shall place the names of the members in a vessel, and draw three names therefrom.

The accused and the Church Advocate may, by a written consent filed with the Secretary of the standing committee, agree upon three Presbyters to form such board. 4

The accused party may at the time of striking such names, or entering into such consent, nominate, in writing, a lay member of the church, being of the profession of the law, to act as an assessor on such trial. If such nomination is made, the Church Advocate may nominate another such assessor ; and the Board of 5

Triers when assembled, may, by a majority of votes, appoint a third. Such board may also appoint a Lay Assessor, whether any have been appointed under this subdivision or not.

The Presbytery and Lay Assessors thus chosen, shall constitute the Board of Triers for the case.

6   The Secretary of the standing committee shall thereupon attest a copy of the presentment, and endorse thereon the names of the selected Presbyters, and of the Lay Assessors, and the nomination of the Church Advocate.

SECTION VI.

Proceedings for and upon the Trial.

Subdivision 1   The Church Advocate shall forthwith transmit such copy of the presentment to the senior presbyter in order of ordination, of the members of such board, who shall be the President thereof. Such President shall appoint a time and place for the trial, of which notice shall be given by the Church Advocate to the accused, and to the other members of the board, which notice shall be served at least thirty days before the time of meeting, or such other time previous as the president shall direct.

The President, in case a commission to examine witnesses is applied for under a provision hereafter made, or for other satisfactory cause, may countermand such notice, and appoint some other time and place for the meeting of the board.

2   The board, or majority of the members, shall have power to adjourn from time to time, and from place to place within the diocese as they shall think proper. If, upon the day appointed for the first meeting, a majority of the members do not attend, any one or more of such members may adjourn over from day to day in his or their discretion, not exceeding two adjournments, nor longer than one day each.

3   The board may appoint a Secretary, either from their own body or otherwise, and a minister or layman.

4   In case of the death, resignation, or refusal to act, or removal from the diocese, of any member of the board, the accused party

and the church advocate may agree upon a member to supply his place. If no such consent is entered into, the party may apply to the President of the standing committee, who shall fill up such vacancy from the other members of the district by lot.

If the accused party do not attend at the time fixed for the trial, 5 or at such time as the same may be adjourned to, unless he shall render a satisfactory excuse to the board for his neglect, the board shall report the fact to the ecclesiastical authority, by which he may be sentenced to be suspended from the exercise of his clerical functions until he shall apply for a trial ; and if, during the period of six months, he shall not apply for a trial, he shall be suspended from the ministry.

The proceedings upon a trial shall be private, unless the accused 6 party shall request that the same be public.

The accused party shall have the privilege of appearing by counsel.

All exceptions to the form, or substance, or legal sufficiency of 7 the presentment, or any part thereof, or of the allegations or specifications therein, or to the jurisdiction of the board, may be taken by the accused, and shall be passed upon by the board.

Such exceptions shall be made in writing, and presented as soon as the board shall be duly organized, or at some future day to be then appointed, upon satisfactory cause shown for the delay.

If no such exceptions are taken, or being taken, are overruled, 8 the accused shall be called upon to answer to each and every charge specifically, guilty or not guilty, and the trial shall proceed.

[When the board shall proceed to trial, it shall hear all such 9 competent evidence as may be produced, which evidence shall be reduced to writing by the Secretary and signed by the witnesses; and some officer authorized by the law of the place in which the trial is had, to administer oaths, may administer an oath or affirmation to the witnesses, in the form used in the civil tribunal of such place.]

If a witness residing within the diocese cannot, from sickness or 10 other satisfactory cause, attend, or if being resident over thirty miles from the place of trial, he refuses to attend in person, the President may appoint a commissioner to take his testimony. Such commissioner may be either a clergyman or layman, and the party applying shall give to the other party at least six days' notice, signed by himself, of the time and place of taking the testimony; and if any person on whom the notice shall be served shall reside more than forty miles from the place of examination, an additional day's notice shall be given for every additional twenty miles of the said distance, and both parties may attend and examine the witness, and the questions and answers shall be reduced to writing and signed by the witness, and shall be certified by the commissioner and transmitted to the board, and be received as evidence.

A witness examined before such commissioner may be sworn or affirmed in the same manner as a witness before the board.

11   At any time within thirty days after the Board of Triers has been selected, the Church Advocate or the accused may apply to the President of such board for a commission to take the testimony of witnesses residing out of the diocese. Ten days' notice thereof shall be given to the opposite party.

The commission shall be under the hand of the President, directed to any presbyter or layman agreed upon between the parties, or selected by the President out of four persons named by the parties, two by each respectively.

The interrogatories of the applicant, and cross-interrogatories of the opposite party, shall be annexed thereto, unless it is agreed in writing and endorsed upon the commission, that the testimony may be orally taken in the presence of the parties, or their agents.

The time and place of executing the same, the notice to be given of such time and place, the mode of the return, and other matters for the proper execution thereof, shall be prescribed by the President, on hearing the parties, and be annexed in the shape of instructions to such commission.

12   If, during the progress of a trial, it shall appear by affidavit, that a material witness resides in another diocese, and the deponent was ignorant of the name of the witness or the matters to which he could depose prior to the first meeting of the board, the board may allow a commission to issue, and adjourn the trial for a sufficient period to allow of its return.

The preceding provisions as to the powers of the President shall apply to this case.

13   If at any time after a charge is made, or an inquiry or trial directed, the accused party shall, by any writing under his hand, confess the truth of the charge, and consent that the ecclesiastical

authority shall forthwith pronounce sentence upon him, such sentence may be pronounced forthwith, as it would be lawful to pronounce, had the offence been duly proven upon a trial ; and such sentence shall bar any further or other proceedings against the party for the same offence.

All notices, citations, papers, or proceedings required to be 14 served upon a minister, shall (unless otherwise specially provided for) be signed by the Ecclesiastical authority of the diocese, or by the Church Advocate, or by the President of the Board of Triers. They shall severally be deemed to be duly served, if a copy thereof is delivered to the minister personally, or is left at his last place of abode within the United States ; and, in case of a citation or notice to appear upon a trial or proceeding, where the minister has departed from the United States, by delivering a copy of such notice or citation to the Secretary of the Standing Committee of the diocese. . And, in such case, the minister shall be cited to appear at the end of six months from the day of such delivery.

Service may be made by a summoner or summoners, to be appointed by the party signing such notice or paper, whose certificate of service shall be evidence thereof.

The lay members of such board shall have equal power with the 15 other members, except that they shall not be entitled to vote upon the final decision, or upon any sentence to be proposed or declared.

The board, upon consideration of the case, shall declare in 16 writing signed by them, or a majority of them, their decision on the charges contained in the presentment ; stating whether the accused is guilty or not guilty of such charges respectively, and also stating the sentence which in their opinion ought to be pronounced. A copy of such decision, together with all their proceedings, including the testimony taken, shall be transmitted to the ecclesiastical authority, before it is transmitted to the accused, or in any way made public. Such authority shall cause a copy of the decision to be transmitted to the accused, except in the case of absence from the diocese.

An application for a new trial may be made within thirty days 17 after the transmission of such copy, or within such further time as such authority will allow.

Such new trial may be granted upon the ground of the rejection of evidence pertinent and material to the case ; or upon newly discovered evidence which it shall be shown was unknown, and could not with reasonable diligence have been known, in time to have been produced at the trial, and upon no other ground.

If a new trial is granted, the same, or a new board may be appointed by the ecclesiastical authority, the proceedings to form, and before which, shall be conducted as before mentioned.

If no new trial is granted, or upon such trial the party shall be convicted, the ecclesiastical authority shall proceed to pronounce such canonical sentence as shall appear proper, and as hereafter regulated, provided that the same shall not exceed in severity the punishment recommended by the court.

SECTION VII.

Proceedings in cases of Heresy and False Doctrine.

Subdi-
vision
1 If a minister is supposed chargeable with any ecclesiastical offence, enumerated in the second subdivision of the First section of this chapter, he shall be proceeded against by presentment only.

The Presentment must be made by three Presbyters of the church canonically resident within the diocese of the accused; or by two Presbyters so resident, and two Presbyters of some other diocese or dioceses. It shall be signed by them, and shall specify the offence, with reasonable certainty as to the time, place, and circumstances. It shall be addressed to the ecclesiastical authority of the diocese, and be delivered to the President of the Standing Committee.

2 The Board of Triers shall consist of Presbyters only, except as hereafter provided. The number shall be five, except in any diocese where the number of Presbyters does not exceed ten, when the number may be three.

Such members shall be selected from the Presbyters of the district in the manner pointed out in the Fifth section of this chapter.

The Church Advocate in such a case shall be a Presbyter named by the standing committee.

3 The court may, by a majority of votes, choose a lay assessor, being a member of the church and of the profession of the law, to sit with and advise them, but without a vote on the decision of any question.

The accused party may appear in person or by a Presbyter selected by him.

The provisions of the fifth and sixth sections of this chapter shall be deemed applicable to proceedings under this section, when not repugnant to any provision of the same.

SECTION VIII.

Record of Proceedings.

Whenever a decision has become final, and sentence has been pronounced, the ecclesiastical authority shall transmit to the Secretary of the Standing Committee of the diocese, all the papers, proceedings, and documents in the case, with the decision and sentence pronounced, attested by such authority; and thereupon the secretary shall make a record of the same in a book to be kept for that purpose.

Such record shall contain a statement of the date of the presentment, the parties to the same, and the charges made therein; the appointment of the Board of Triers, and names of the members; the date, and a transcript of the decision of such board; the subsequent proceedings by way of appeal or otherwise, if any, and the final decision and sentence pronounced, in full.

SECTION IX.

Rules by Ecclesiastical Authority.

The Ecclesiastical authority of each diocese, by and with the advice and consent of the standing committee thereof, may make such orders and regulations as shall be deemed advisable, for the better carrying out the purposes of this chapter, provided the same are not inconsistent with any of the provisions hereof, or with the constitution, or canons of this church : provided also, that the same be reported to the ensuing General Convention.

CHAPTER II.

OF APPEALS.

SECTION I.

The Right of Appeal.

Subdivision 1. Any minister of this church who has been found guilty upon any proceedings had under the fourth section of the first chapter of this canon, may appeal from such finding and decision, to the Appellate Court of the diocese hereinafter constituted.

2. In cases of proceedings had under the seventh section of such first chapter, an appeal may be had from the judgment or sentence of the ecclesiastical authority of the diocese where the trial has been had, to the Court of Bishops, as provided in the sixth section of this chapter.

SECTION II.

Diocesan Appellate Court.

Subdivision 1. At the next annual meeting of the several diocesan conventions of this church to be held after the adoption of this canon, or at the meetiug next ensuing such meeting, each ccnvention shall appoint (in such manner as they shall see fit) seven presbyters, and seven laymen of the profession of the law, who shall be, and be known, as members of the Appellate Court of such diocese.

It shall be lawful, however, for any diocese, in which the number of presbyters does not exceed twenty, and exceeds ten, to choose a smaller number of both orders, or either order, as such members, provided that not less than three presbyters and three laymen be chosen. In any diocese where the number of presbyters is ten or less, the establishment of such a court may be omitted in the discretion of the convention, until ten presbyters be canonically resident therein. (*a*)

2. The tenure of the office of the members shall be three years from the date of their appointment. It shall be the duty of the several conventions to fill in succession the places of all the members whose terms of office have expired. In case of an omission so to do, the members shall continue in office until others shall be appointed in their stead. Vacancies occurring during the recess of the convention may be filled by the remaining members ; the persons nominated to continue in office until the action of the convention, or the expiration of three years, under the same provision as is made as to other members.

3. The members of such court shall meet together as soon as convenient after their appointment, and shall choose one of their number, being a presbyter, for president, and another, being a layman, for secretary ; and upon being so organized they shall be, and be known as " The Appellate Court for the diocese of ———, as the case may be.

Such president and secretary shall respectively hold their office during the term of their office as members of the court ; and upon vacancies occurring, others may be appointed in their place, by the members.

SECTION III.

Mode of Appealing.

1. The Ecclesiastical authority of the diocese within which proceedings and a trial have been had, shall in no case proceed to pronounce sentence until the expiration of thirty days from the reception of the finding and decision of the Board of Triers, nor without satisfactory proof that a copy of the decision has been delivered to the accused.

(*a*) In a small diocese of six or eight presbyters, it would be impracticable or difficult to form a Board of Triers and an Appellate Court of different persons. The inconvenience in such cases will be but transient.

2. Within thirty days after the notice of the finding and decision of such board has been served, the party may file his appeal.

3. Such appeal shall be in writing, setting out the decision, and specifying that the party appeals from such decision or from some part thereof, and what part; and shall be addressed to the president of the appellate court of the diocese within which the trial has been had.

4. A copy thereof shall be delivered to the ecclesiastical authority and another to the church advocate in the case. The return of the Board of Triers with such appeal shall thereupon be transmitted by the ecclesiastical authority to the Secretary of the standing committe.

5. A copy of such appeal and of the return of the Board of Triers shall be transmitted to the president of the said appellate court, at the cost of the appellant. Such copy shall be certified by the secretary of the standing committee.

6. The ecclesiastical authority of the diocese within which the trial has been had, may extend the time for taking such appeal, by a certificate in writing, but not to exceed thirty additional days.

SECTION IV.

Striking off Names.

Whenever there are four or more members of each order of such appellate court, the president shall forthwith upon the receipt of such appeal give notice to the accused and the church advocate to attend before him at a designated time and place, to select the members to hear the appeal. At such time and place the accused in person or by his agent may first strike off one of each order from the list of members, and the church advocate another, and so alternately, until the list is reduced to three of each order.

SECTION V.

The Hearing.

I. The president of the appellate court, shall forthwith upon the receipt of such appeal, give notice in writing thereof to the several members of the court, and to the church advocate, and shall in such notice appoint a time and place for the meeting of the court to hear such appeal. He shall also have power to change such time and place, causing reasonable notice of such change to be given to the said appellant and church advocate.

2. The court shall consist of all the members of such appellate court, except those whose names may have been struck off in the manner pointed out in the preceding section.

In case the number is reduced to three of either order, and any member is unable to attend from sickness, or other cause satisfactory to the President of the court, the latter shall place the names of the other members of such order in a vessel, and in the presence of the parties draw a member to supply the place.

3. At the time and place appointed, if the whole number of members constituting the appellate court in the case, do not attend, the members present may adjourn to another time, not exceeding three days.

4. If the President or Secretary of the appellate court be not one of the members to hear the case, those present may choose a President or Secretary for such case.

5. If the President of such court be the accused party, the eldest presbyter in the order of ordination shall be the President of such court for all the purposes of this section.

6. If after the hearing of the appeal has commenced, any of the members present shall be unable to proceed from sickness, or other cause satisfactory to a majority of the members, the hearing of the case may nevertheless be concluded, provided three presbyters and two laymen shall continue to hear it.

7. The hearing shall be in the presence of the church advocate, and of the appellant and his counsel only, unless otherwise desired by the appellant.

8. The lay members of the Board shall have equal power with the other members, except that they shall not be entitled to vote upon the final decision of the appeal.

9. The court may reverse the decision of the Board of Triers in whole or in part, or may modify the sentence proposed to be pronounced, provided either—that all the clerical members present (if the number shall not exceed three) vote therefor; and if such number exceed three, then that two-thirds of such number vote therefor. In all other cases, as well as upon a default of the appellant, the decision shall be affirmed.

10. The decision of the court shall be endorsed upon or annexed to the appeal; and the same, together with all the papers made use of upon the hearing, shall be transmitted to the Ecclesiastical authority of the Diocese, for revision and final determination and judgment.

11. The Secretary of the appellate court shall transcribe into a book to be kept for that purpose, the appeal with a minute of the proceedings of the court, and the decision, and shall subscribe and attest the same.

12. The ecclesiastical authority, after pronouncing the final decision and sentence in the case, shall transmit all the papers, with a minute of such decision, to the Secretary of the standing committee, whose duty it shall be to record an abstract of the proceedings and the final sentence at length, in a book kept for that purpose.

SECTION VI.

Miscellaneous.

The Ecclesiastical authority of the Diocese, by and with the advice and consent of the standing committee thereof, may make such orders and regulations as shall be deemed advisable, for the better carrying into effect the foregoing provisions of this chapter; provided the same are not inconsistent therewith, nor contrary to the constitution and canons of this church.

It shall be the duty of such authority to report to the general convention any proceedings which have been had under the first and second chapters of this canon, with such suggestions for the amendment thereof as may be deemed expedient.

SECTION VII.

Appeals to Courts of Bishops.

The term " Bishop," for the purposes of this section, shall be construed to mean— _{Subdi-vision 1}

A Bishop of a Diocese in full authority and charge thereof.

An Assistant or Provisional Bishop.

A Missionary Bishop appointed to exercise Episcopal functions within States or Territories not organized into Dioceses.

The Dioceses of the Protestant Episcopal Church in the United States of America, shall, for the purposes of this canon be arranged into four Collegiate Dioceses. 2

The first Collegiate Diocese shall consist of the Dioceses of Maine, New Hampshire, Massachusetts, Vermont, Rhode Island, Connecticut, Western New York, and New York.

The second, of the Dioceses of New Jersey, Pennsylvania, Delaware, Maryland, Virginia, North Carolina, South Carolina, and Georgia.

The third, of the Dioceses of Florida, Alabama, Mississippi, Louisiana, Kentucky, Texas, Tennessee, and the State of Arkansas.

The fourth, of the Dioceses of Indiana, Illinois, Ohio, Michigan, Missouri, and the States or Territories of Wisconsin, Iowa, and Minesota.

Upon the formation of a new Diocese under the authority of the General Convention, it shall be declared by such Convention to which of such Collegiate Dioceses the same shall belong.

The Bishops in each of such Collegiate Dioceses respectively, shall form an appellate court, to be, and to be known, as " The Court of Bishops for the—Collegiate Diocese " as the case may be. 3 The eldest Bishop in such Collegiate Diocese, in the order of consecration, shall be the President of such court, and it shall be his duty to convene the members thereof at some suitable time and place, for the purpose of choosing a Secretary. Such Secretary may be either a minister, or layman, in the discretion of such court.

If it shall be inconvenient for any member to attend at the time and place appointed, his nomination in writing of a Secretary shall be, for the purpose of a choice, as valid as if he were present.

4   An appeal may be taken from the judgment and sentence of the ecclesiastical authority of any Diocese within a Collegiate Diocese, to the Court of Bishops thereof, in the cases of proceedings under the seventh section of the first chapter of this canon, entitled " Proceedings in cases of Heresy and False Doctrine," and in no other cases.

5   Such appeal shall be in writing, addressed to the President of such court, unless the appeal is from his decision, when it shall be addressed to the eldest, in the order of consecration, of the other Bishops, who shall be the President for the particular case.

The appeal shall set forth the decision, and sentence to be pronounced ; stating that the party appeals from the same, or from some designated part thereof.

Such appeal must be taken within thirty days after notice of the decision and sentence intended to be pronounced, which notice shall be given to the accused by the ecclesiastical authority of the Diocese. Such authority shall not proceed to carry the sentence into effect until the expiration of such thirty days.

6   The fourth, fifth, and sixth subdivisions of the third section of this chapter, shall apply to cases of appeals taken under this section. In addition to the documents specified in such fifth section, the decision and proposed sentence of the ecclesiastical authority shall be annexed.

7   The President of the court, upon receiving such appeal, shall give notice thereof to the other Bishops of such Collegiate Diocese, and shall appoint a time and place for the hearing of the same. He shall cause notice of such appointment to be given to the appellant, and also to the ecclesiastical authority of the Diocese, whose decision is appealed from.

Four Bishops shall form a quorum for hearing and deciding such appeal. The Bishop from whose decision the appeal is taken, shall not be a member of the court.

8   The Church Advocate, if a Presbyter, may attend the court and discuss the case. If there is no church advocate, the ecclesiastical authority of the Diocese in which the decision has been made, may appoint a Presbyter to act as Church Advocate in the case. The accused party shall be heard in person, or by such Presbyter as he shall appoint.

The decision may be made by a majority of the members of the court present.

The Secretary shall enter of record the names of the Bishops and their votes respectively, with the decision. He shall endorse the same upon the appeal, or annex it thereto.

Such appeal, with all the documents used in the Court of Appeal annexed thereto, shall be transmitted to the ecclesiastical authority of the Diocese for action thereon. And such authority shall deliver the same to the Secretary of the standing committee, who shall make the record thereof as prescribed in the eighth section of the first chapter of this canon.

SECTION VIII.

Appeals to the Bench of Bishops.

1. In case the sentence appealed from to the Court of Bishops, established under the seventh section of this chapter, shall be affirmed by any number of Bishops less than four, (*a*) or in case the said appellate court is equally divided, or the sentence to be pronounced is degradation, an appeal may be taken by the accused to the whole bench of Bishops.

In case the sentence is reversed by any number of Bishops less than four, the ecclesiastical authority, whose sentence is appealed from, may, in like manner, appeal to such bench of Bishops.

2. The appeal shall be in writing signed by the appellant, and setting forth the judgment or sentence complained of. It shall be addressed to the presiding Bishop of this Church, and shall be lodged with the secretary of the Court of Bishops.

3. Such secretary shall certify the record brought into the said court of Bishops by appeal, and shall add thereto the judgment or sentence of such court, and shall cause the same to be transmitted at the expense of the appellant, to the presiding Bishop of this Church.

(*a*) That is, if five Bishops including the Diocesan, unite in a sentence, there shall be no further appeal.

9

4. A majority of all the Diocesan Bishops of this Church, not including the Bishop whose judgment was first appealed from, nor the Bishops who heard the appeal, shall be necessary to form a quorum to hear the appeal; Provided, that an Assistant Bishop may be a member of such court, whenever his Diocesan does not attend.

5. A majority of all the Bishops who shall hear the appeal, shall be sufficient to affirm the judgment or sentence. A vote of two-thirds shall be necessary to reverse the same.

6. The record of the decision shall be annexed to the record of the proceedings below, and shall be transmitted by the Secretary, to the Secretary of the standing committee of the Diocese where the case originated.

7 The presiding Bishop for the time being, with the consent of any six Bishops of the Church, may from time to time, make and establish all orders and regulations necessary or convenient for the convening of such bench of Bishops, the time and place thereof, respecting adjournments, the mode of proceeding, and as to any other matters proper for the assembling, and the conduct of the business, thereof.

Such orders and regulations shall be subject to the revision of the Bishops when assembled as a House of Bishops, or for hearing an appeal.

CHAPTER III.

OF THE TRIAL OF A BISHOP.

SECTION I.

Definition of Terms.

Subdivision.
1
Except when it shall otherwise appear from the context, the term " Bishop " within the provisions, and for the purposes of this chapter, shall be construed to mean :—

The Bishop of a Diocese in full authority and charge thereof:

An Assistant Bishop:

A Provisional Bishop:

A Missionary Bishop, whether appointed to exercise Episcopal functions within States or Territories not organized into Dioceses, or exercising such functions in any missionary station or stations of this church out of the territory of the United States.

A Missionary Bishop out of the territory of the United States,   2 shall for the purposes of this chapter be deemed a resident of the diocese, in which he was last canonically resident when a Presbyter.

Of Punishable Offences.

The Ecclesiastical offences for which a Bishop is liable to presentment, trial, and punishment, are those enumerated in the first and second sub-divisions of the second section of Chapter I. of this Canon. The other sub-divisions of the same section shall apply to this case.

Who may Present.

The power of presenting a Bishop is vested in the Board of Enquiry hereinafter designated; in the Convention of the diocese to which he belongs; and in a Bishop of the Church as hereinafter provided.

Commissioners of Inquiry.

The members of the Standing Committee in each diocese within Subdivision 1 the several collegiate dioceses, established under the seventh section of the second chapter hereof, shall, for the purposes of this chapter, be entitled to act as Commissioners of Inquiry for such Collegiate Diocese, upon a charge against a Bishop resident within the same, under the following provisions :—

Each Standing Committee shall, as soon as convenient after   2 their election by the respective Conventions, select one Presbyter and one Layman from among their number, who shall be and be known as Commissioners of Inquiry for such diocese.

3   The said Committee may fill any vacancy which may occur in such nomination, by reason of death, removal from the diocese, a written resignation, or a canonical disability.

4   Such Commissioners shall continue in office so long as they remain members of the Standing Committee appointing them; unless such Committee provide by order for some other term of service, or for the service of each of their members, as such Commissioners, in rotation; which they are hereby empowered to do.

5   In any diocese in which there are no lay members of the Standing Committee, two Presbyters shall be selected by the said Committee, unless the Convention shall make provision for the appointment of Laymen to act under this section.

6   The Secretary of the Standing Committee of each Diocese within the respective Collegiate Dioceses, shall forthwith transmit to the Secretary of such Committee of each other diocese within the same, the names and places of residence of the members so selected as Commissioners, and shall transmit a similar notice from time to time, upon any other members being selected. Each Secretary shall make a record of such names and residences in a book kept for that purpose.

7   The members thus selected in the several dioceses shall be and be known as " Commissioners of Inquiry for the Collegiate Diocese," as the case may be.

SECTION V.

The Charge.

Subdivision 1   An accusation of a Bishop for any ecclesiastical offence, enumerated in the first sub-division of the second section of the first chapter of this canon, shall be made in writing in the form of a charge, in which shall be specified the offences of which he is alleged to be guilty.

The same shall be stated with reasonable certainty as to the time and place of the commission of such offences.

It shall be addressed to " The Commissioners of Inquiry for 2 the   Collegiate Diocese," as the case may be, and shall be delivered to any one of such Commissioners, being a presbyter, within such Collegiate Diocese, other than a presbyter residing in the diocese to which the accused Bishop belongs.

It shall be signed either by four presbyters of this Church, ca- 3 nonically resident within the diocese of the accused ; or by three presbyters so resident, and two laymen communicants of the church, and residents therein ; or by three presbyters, and three laymen communicants of this church, and residents within the collegiate diocese.

It shall be accompanied by the oath or affirmation of the par- 4 ties making it, that they know the charge stated therein to be true, or that they have carefully and impartially examined the statements and information of others, upon which such charge is founded, and believe the same to be true.

It shall be accompanied with the affidavits or affirmations of one 5 or more persons, (except where the accusers swear of their own knowledge to the facts,) stating the facts and circumstances tending to prove the charge, with reasonable precision as to time and place, and also with any documentary evidence in the power of the accusers to produce.

The accusers shall indorse on such charge, the name of a church, 6 advocate to appear on their behalf, who shall be a layman, and member of this church.

SECTION VI.

The Mode of Enquiry.

The presbyter to whom such charge shall be delivered, shall di- Subdivision rect the accusers to furnish him with a copy of the same, and 1 shall transmit such copy to the accused Bishop, with a list of all the Commissioners of Enquiry within such Collegiate Diocese, and their places of residence ; which list shall be certified and furnished by the Secretary of the Standing Committee in the diocese of such presbyter.

He shall also designate a time and place at which the accused 2 and the church advocate may appear to strike names from such list. The accused Bishop, and the church advocate, or some one on their behalf respectively, may at such time and place, strike from such list alternately, the names of such members as they think fit, until the number of each order is reduced to four.

The Commissioners whose names are not so struck off shall constitute the Board of Inquiry in the case. The eldest presbyter in the order of ordination shall be the President thereof; and the church advocate shall forthwith transmit the original charge, with the list of the members of the Board of Inquiry, to such presbyter.

3   The provisions of the first, second, third, fourth, sixth, seventh, eighth, ninth, tenth, eleventh, twelfth and fourteenth sub-divisions of the sixth section of the first chapter of this canon, with necessary variations of style and form, shall apply in proceedings taken under this section.

4   The question shall be, whether the charge has been sufficiently established by the evidence produced, as to warrant a presentment. A majority of each order shall vote in the affirmative, or the charge shall be dismissed.

5   If the Commissioners decide to present, they may forthwith appoint one of their number to prepare with the church advocate such presentment. They shall also designate the church advocate before them, or some other layman being a member of the church, to be the church advocate upon future proceedings. And they may appoint an associate church advocate if they shall see fit, being a lay member of the church. The presentment shall be signed by all the Commissioners concurring in the same.

SECTION VII.

Enquiry by a Convention.

Subdivison. 1   If the Board of Enquiry dismiss the charge by a unanimous vote, or by a unanimous vote of the clerical members, and a majority of the lay members, the decision shall be final, and equivalent to an acquittal upon all the matters of such charge. If the dismissal is upon a vote less than that above mentioned, the Diocesan Convention shall be at liberty to receive the charge and to act thereupon; provided the same is brought before it at the next Convention ensuing such dismissal, if two months shall elapse before the meeting of the same, or at the meeting of the next ensuing Convention thereafter.

The accusers may thereupon procure a certified copy of the **2** accusation and of all the evidence taken before the Board of Enquiry, with the decision and the vote thereupon, from the Secretary, and shall cause the same to be delivered to the Secretary of the Diocesan Convention. It shall be the duty of such Secretary to acquaint the Convention of his receipt of the same ; or any number may call for the reading thereof.

" The said accusation shall lie on the table of the Convention for **3** one day, Sunday not being considered a day for such purpose. It shall then be lawful for any member of the Convention to move a resolution that the charges be disregarded ; the question on such resolution shall be taken by orders, and shall be lost, unless three-fifths of each order present shall concur. If no such resolution is moved, or if it be lost, it shall be the duty of the Convention to appoint a Committee of Enquiry."

The Record of the Board of Enquiry shall be delivered **4** to such committee. Such committee shall not re-examine any witness before examined, except to matters as to which he has not previously deposed. Nor shall any fresh testimony be admitted, except upon affidavit of the party offering it, that it has been discovered since the hearing of testimony was closed before the Board. They shall give notice to the accusers and to the accused Bishop of the time and places of their meeting ; they shall report the evidence and their proceedings to the Convention, at an adjourned meeting to be held, not less than thirty, nor more than sixty days after the appointment of the Committee. The persons so notified shall have a right to be present at all such meetings, to produce and examine witnesses, with the qualifications above mentioned, and to cross-examine witnesses produced on the other side."

" At such adjourned meeting, no business touching the charges **5** shall be done, until it has been ascertained that two-thirds of the clergy entitled to seats in the Convention, and a representation of two-thirds of the parishes canonically in union with the same, are present. If a motion be then made to present, it shall not be regarded as carried unless a number of votes equal to a majority of the votes previously ascertained to have been present, shall be given in its favor."

6   When it is determined to make a presentment, it shall be drawn up in writing, and signed by a committee of three laymen and three clergymen, appointed by the Convention. Such committee shall appoint one of their number to act as Church Advocate in the case, or may re-appoint the former Church Advocate.

7   The refusal of a Diocesan Convention to present shall be considered as a full and final acquittal, as to the charges brought before them.

SECTION VIII.

Court for the Trial.

Subdivision. 1   The provisions of this section relate only to proceedings under a presentment by the authority of a Board of enquiry, or of a diocesan convention.

2   The Bishops of the dioceses designated as belonging to the first and second collegiate dioceses, in the seventh section of the second chapter of this canon, entitled, "Appeals to courts of Bishops," shall constitute one class for the trial of an accused Bishop; and the Bishops of the dioceses designated as belonging to the third and fourth collegiate dioceses shall constitute another class for such trial.

3   A Bishop belonging to any diocese within the two first collegiate dioceses, shall be amenable to the Bishops thereof; and a Bishop belonging to any diocese within the two last collegiate dioceses, shall be amenable to the Bishops thereof.

4   The Presentment shall be addressed to the eldest Bishop, in the order of consecration, in such collegiate dioceses respectively, and shall be delivered to him by the church advocate. Such Bishop shall thereupon direct the church advocate to serve a copy of the presentment upon the accused, with a notice to attend at a time and place to be fixed by him for the purpose of selecting the members of the court. Such notice must be served at least thirty days before the time appointed. Due proof of the service shall be furnished to such Bishop.

5   At the time specified, the accused and the church advocate, or their respective agents, may attend, and the accused may strike

off the list of such Bishops as are herein authorized to try him, one name, and the church advocate another, and so on alternately until the number is reduced to nine, who shall compose the court.

If both parties, or either party, fail to attend, the Bishop may adjourn, if he think proper, to the next or some other day, and if one of the parties only then attend, may proceed to strike off so many names designated by the attending party as he would have been entitled to strike off, had the other party joined therein.

All the Bishops belonging to dioceses within such two collegiate dioceses, whose names are not struck off, shall be deemed members of the court for the trial.

The Bishop to whom the presentment has been addressed shall 6 be the president of such court, unless his name has been struck off; in which case the eldest Bishop, in the order of consecration, of the Bishops of the court, shall be such president.

The Presentment, proof of service, with a list of the members 7 of the court, attested by the Bishop to whom the presentment has been addressed, shall be delivered to the president of the court. Such president shall thereupon appoint a time and place for the trial, which place shall be within the diocese of the accused, and which time shall be at least thirty days from the service of the notice. The church advocate shall cause a notice thereof to be served on the accused, and shall furnish due proof of such service. Notice shall in like manner be given by him to all the Bishops who compose the court.

Such Bishops, or any seven or eight of them, assembled at the 8 time and place appointed, shall constitute the court for the trial of the accused.

The accused may at such time and place, before the trial is 9 commenced, name a lay assessor, a member of the church and of the profession of the law, to sit in such court; and in such case, but in such case only, the church advocate may name another. The court may appoint a lay assessor as aforesaid in every case, whether any one has been appointed by the parties or not.

Such lay assessors shall have a vote upon all questions, except upon the final decision or judgment of the court.

The court may appoint a secretary, either one of their number 10 or not, and either a presbyter or layman.

10

11   If the accused Bishop appear, he shall, before proceeding to trial, be called upon by the court to say, whether he is guilty or not guilty of the offence or offences charged against him,—and on his neglect or refusal to do so, the plea of not guilty shall be entered for him, and the trial shall proceed.

12   The Court may, for sufficient cause, adjourn from time to time. If after the trial has commenced any member or members should die, or be unable to attend, from sickness, or unavoidable impediment of which the Court shall judge, the trial may nevertheless proceed, provided that not less than six bishops continue to hear the same.

13   The record of the testimony taken before the Board of Enquiry, or a Committee of the Convention, or both, shall be brought by the Church Advocate into the Court, and deposited with the Secretary. It may be used as evidence before the Court.

14   All the provisions of the sixth section of the first chapter of this canon, entitled—" Proceedings for and upon the Trial," with the necessary variations of form and style, shall apply to proceedings under this section, except where there are other provisions upon the subject matter herein, and except that in case of contumacy of the accused under the fifth subdivision of such section, the Court shall declare the sentence.

15   The Court having fully heard the allegations and proofs of the parties, and deliberately considered the same, shall declare respectively whether in their opinion the accused is guilty or not guilty of each particular charge contained in the presentment; and also which of the several specifications therein is proven, and which not proven. The specifications which are not declared proven by a vote of two-thirds of the members of the Court shall be considered as not proven, and the accused shall be deemed not guilty upon the charges as to which he is not pronounced guilty. The record of the Court shall be made according to this provision.

16   If the accused has been found guilty, the Court may give him time to be heard before passing sentence ; and shall appoint a time for pronouncing the same, and shall hear what he has to say in excuse or palliation. At that time an application may be made for a further hearing ; but only on the ground stated in an affidavit or affirmation, of the discovery of new evidence material to the

case, which was not known to the party, and could not with reasonable diligence have been known. (*a.*) In such case the Court may appoint another day to hear such further testimony, and to have the case re-argued.

The Court shall then proceed to declare the sentence to be pronounced.

Such sentence shall not be pronounced until the expiration of 17 sixty days from the date of the decision, at which time if no appeal has been taken as is hereafter provided for, the presiding Bishop of the Court (or in case of his death or inability, the next Bishop in the order of consecration, a member of such Court) shall pronounce and declare the sentence in the manner pointed cut in the third section of the title " Miscellaneous Provisions," hereafter contained.

SECTION IX.

Appeal to the Bench of Bishops.

Whenever a Bishop has been found guilty of any Ecclesiastical 1 offence, upon a trial had under the preceding sections of this chapter, and the decision has been made by any number less than six Bishops, members of the Court ; or wherever the sentence to be pronounced is deposition, an appeal may be taken to the whole Bench of Bishops.

The appeal shall be in writing, stating the decision or part of 2 the decision appealed from. It shall be signed by the appellant, and addressed to the Presiding Bishop of the Church. A copy thereof shall be transmitted to him, and another copy filed with the Secretary of the Court, by which the case was tried. Such appeal shall be taken within sixty days after the decision of the Court.

(*a*) It strikes me that the Project of a canon (§ 24) is in the particular of a new trial, too liberal. After a case has been sifted as it would be on a preliminary enquiry, then on a full trial, justice does not seem to require a further litigation.

3   The Secretary shall thereupon, at the expense of the appellant, transmit to the Presiding Bishop the Record containing the presentment, proceedings, testimony, and decision.

4   The sixth, seventh, and eighth sub-divisions of the sixth section of chapter I. of this canon, with the necessary variations of style and form, shall apply to proceedings under this section.

5   The powers given to the presiding Bishop of the Church, with the concurrence of six Bishops, in and by the seventh sub-division of the eighth section of the second chapter of this canon, may be exercised by such Bishop in like manner, in relation to cases under this section.

SECTION X.

Presentment of a Bishop for Heresy and False Doctrine.

1   An accusation against a Bishop for any Ecclesiastical offence within the second subdivision of the second section of Chapter I. of this canon, shall be made by a Presentment as hereafter provided, and in no other mode.

2   It shall be made by any Bishop in communion with this Church, residing in the United States, and not at the time under degradation or suspension.   It shall not be lawful for two or more Bishops to unite in any such presentment.   (Project of a Canon.)

3   Such presentment shall be signed by the Bishop making it, and shall, if the heretical or erroneous doctrine be contained in any printed book, pamphlet, or paper, contain a description of such book, pamphlet or paper, and be accompanied by a copy thereof; and shall distinctly specify the passages which are complained of. If the heretical or erroneous doctrines be not contained in any printed book, pamphlet or paper, it shall be specified with reasonable certainty. (Ibid.)

4   If the erroneous or heretical doctrine presented shall not be contained in any book, pamphlet or paper, published with the name or signature of the accused Bishop, it shall be lawful for the accused to deny in writing, with his signature, that he has taught or holds the doctrine objected against him.   Such denial shall be conclusive, as far as the presentment is concerned; but if it be

untrue, in the point of denying the teaching, it may itself be the subject of a presentment for immorality. If the heretical or erroneous doctrine be contained in any book, pamphlet or paper, published with the signature or name of the accused Bishop, such book, pamphlet or paper shall be *prima facie* proof of its authorship. If the accused Bishop shall not deny his having taught the doctrine complained of in the presentment, or shall be unable to disprove the authorship of the book, pamphlet or paper published with his name or signature, the issue shall be considered as joined on the question, whether the doctrine complained of be heretical or erroneous. (Ibid.)

Such presentment shall be transmitted to the presiding Bishop, 5 and the accuser may at the same time name a Church Advocate, being a presbyter. The Presiding Bishop shall direct the presenter or advocate to cause a copy thereof to be served on the accused, and to transmit to him the evidence of such service.

If it shall be deemed necessary on the part of the presenter or 6 accused to take testimony, notice may be given within sixty days after such service, of an application to the presiding Bishop, to appoint commissioners for that purpose. Twenty days notice of such application shall be served on the opposite party. The respective parties may attend in person or by an agent. The presiding Bishop shall receive nominations of commissioners from each party if offered, and shall select or appoint two presbyters, and one layman being a member of the church to take such testimony. The eldest presbyter in the order of ordination shall preside. Such commissioners shall appoint a time and place for taking the evidence, and shall give notice thereof to the parties.

The commissioners shall have power to adjourn from time to time and from place to place. The witnesses may be sworn by any officer authorized to administer oaths or affirmations by the laws of the state, territory, or place, in which the testimony is taken.

The record of the testimony taken shall be transmitted to the presiding Bishop. Copies may be furnished to the parties at their expense, to be certified by the presiding presbyter.

At the expiration of sixty days after receiving such present- 7 ment, and due proof of service thereof, by the presiding Bishop, or after the expiration of thirty days after the return of such testimony as may be taken, the case shall be deemed ready for trial.

8   The sixth, seventh, and eighth sub-divisions of the sixth section of Chapter I. of this canon, with the necessary variations of the style and form, shall apply to proceedings under this section.

9   The powers given to the presiding Bishop, with the concurrence of six Bishops of the church, in and by the seventh sub-division of the eighth section of the second chapter of this canon, may be exercised by such Bishop in like manner, in relation to cases under this section.

MISCELLANEOUS PROVISIONS.

SECTION I.

Of Witnesses Refusing to Testify, &c.

1   If any member of the church shall be summoned to attend as a witness before any Board of Triers, Board of Enquiry, Court, Commissioners, or Committee of a Convention, constituted under any provision of this canon, or being present before either of the same, shall refuse to testify, or to be sworn or affirmed, such a person may be declared guilty of contumacy and punished therefor.

2   A certificate of the facts and of the neglect or omission, shall be signed by the president of the Board, Court, or by the Commissioner, or the chairman of the committee, as the case may be.

3   Where the proceedings are under any provision contained in the two first chapters of this canon, such certificate shall be delivered to the ecclesiastical authority of the diocese where such proceedings are had.

When the proceedings are under any provision contained in the third chapter of this canon, the certificate shall be delivered to any Bishop of the church belonging to the collegiate diocese, within which the proceedings are had, who shall be the ecclesiastical authority in the matter.

Such ecclesiastical authority shall thereupon cause reasonable notice to be given to the party of the proceeding intended against him ; and upon hearing the allegations, may proceed, if the party is a layman, to admonish or suspend him from the communion of the church, and if a minister or Bishop, to admonish or suspend him from office.

Such suspension shall continue, and shall be declared to continue, until a satisfactory profession of repentance has been submitted to the ecclesiastical authority, to which the witness has become amenable. (a)   5

SECTION II.
Application to Civil Tribunals.

If at any time pending proceedings against a minister or Bishop   1 under any of the provisions of this canon, an application shall be

(a) The provisions upon this subject which I have met with are the following :— Bishop Hopkins, in the 4th section of his proposed canon of 1847, provided, that the party should be suspended *ipso facto* from the communion of the church, until a satisfactory confession of repentence be submitted to the Bishop to whose jurisdiction the witness is amenable.

In the 5th section of the canon proposed in 1850, for the trial of Bishops (adopted in the 21st section of the Project,) the provision is that the person so refusing to testify, &c., may be sentenced by the court in a summary manner to admonition ; and the sentence of admonition shall be drawn up in such form as the court shall approve, and read during divine service by the officiating minister, in such place or places of worship as the court shall direct ; and it is hereby made the duty of every clergyman of this church to obey the directions of the court in the matter.

The canon of Massachusetts, as reported in May, 1853, provides, that such person so refusing to testify, if he be a clergyman, shall be liable for contumacy. It has no provision as to laymen.

By a canon of Archbishop Boniface, laymen shall be compelled by excommunication, if need be, to take an oath to speak the truth, when enquiry shall be made by the presbyters and judges ecclesiastical, for the corrections of sins and excesses, (Apud Burns, vol. 3, p. 14.)

The object of a provision of this nature is to infuse into the minds of the members of the church, and to keep before them, a sense of the duty of giving, in the courts of justice, such information as they possess. It is also to provide a suitable punishment for those who advisedly and injuriously neglect this duty. I doubt if a public admonition in the time of service is expedient to produce this effect. I doubt, also, whether it is serviceable to the temper of mind befitting a place of worship, that these business notices should be extended. A private course would, I should think, be more serviceable.

made by him for the interposition of any civil tribunal, to stay or delay such proceedings, an affidavit or affirmation of the fact may be made and laid before the ecclesiastical authority.

2   In all proceedings had under the two first chapters of this canon, such authority shall be the ecclesiastical authority of the diocese of the accused. In proceedings under the third chapter hereof, it shall be a Bishop of any diocese within the Collegiate Diocese to which the accused Bishop belongs.

3   Such authority shall summon the party at a reasonable time to attend, and if the proceedings are not, within a time to be specified, discontinued in due form of law, may pronounce a sentence of suspension to remain in force until such discontinuance is made.

4   After such suspension is pronounced, the party shall not be allowed to attend in person, or by counsel, or agent, upon any subsequent proceedings upon the offence alleged against him.

5   This section shall not be construed to prevent an application to the civil tribunals, after a final decision has been pronounced in the case, by action for malicious prosecution, slander, or otherwise, now permitted by the rules of law ; nor to affect in any way such application for the purpose of determining rights or claims in or to property of any description, and the effect of such sentence upon the same. (a)

SECTION III.

Of Sentences.

1   The censure and sentences known in this church for ecclesiastical offences, are admonition, degradation, and excommunication.

Neither of these sentences shall be pronounced upon any presbyter or deacon, by any person other than a Bishop. Admonition and suspension may be pronounced by a presbyter upon a layman.

2   Admonition of a minister for any ecclesiastical offence, not made a subject for judicial inquiry or presentment, shall be made by

---

(a) See Appendix, Note VI.

the Ecclesiastical authority in private. Upon a second offence, it shall be public or private, in the discretion of such authority ; and made in such a manner as the said authority shall think proper.

Admonition, when recommended or declared as the proper sentence, by a board or court, instituted for the trial of an ecclesiastical offence of a Bishop or minister, may be public or private, as such board shall recommend, and the Ecclesiastical authority shall approve, or as such court shall determine.

Whenever the penalty of suspension shall be inflicted on any 3 Bishop, priest, or deacon in this church, the sentence shall specify on what terms, or at what time the penalty shall cease.

Suspension from the exercise of the functions of the ministry, 4 shall *ipso facto* sever the connection between the minister so suspended and his parish or congregation, unless otherwise provided for in such sentence. This provision shall extend to the case of a Bishop holding a rectorship or cure. Such severance shall be declared in the sentence.

(*Or.*) [In every sentence of suspension, it shall be declared, whether the same shall sever the connection between the minister and his parish or congregation, or not. If the same is declared therein not severed, yet it shall be deemed interrupted during the operation of the sentence : and in such case the Ecclesiastical authority, and if there is none within the diocese, the Standing Committee, may authorize any minister to perform ministerial duties in such parish or congregation during such suspension.]

[In such case it is declared, that by the law of this church the wardens and vestrymen of the parish or church may appropriate the whole or such part of the salary, profits or emoluments attached to the office of minister or rector, as they shall think proper, for the support of the minister invited to perform such ministerial duties. Provided however, that the assent of the suspended minister or rector be given thereto in writing. And in case, upon a written application for such consent, the same be refused or withheld, then upon due proof thereof, the Ecclesiastical authority may proceed to declare the connection wholly severed. Provided also, that the amount to be appropriated shall be subject to the revision of the Ecclesiastical authority, with the advice and consent of the Standing Committee.]

11

5   When any minister is degraded from the holy ministry, he is degraded therefrom entirely, and not from a higher to a lower order of the same. Deposition, displacing, and all like expressions are the same as degradation. No degraded minister shall be restored to the ministry.

6   Upon a sentence of degradation being pronounced upon any Bishop or Minister, the connection between such Bishop or Minister, and his parish or congregation, is *ipso facto* severed ; and all offices which he holds by virtue of his office or otherwise, under any canon of this church, or of any diocese, shall wholly cease and determine ; and in case of a sentence of suspension, the said offices shall not be exercised during the continuance of such sentence.

7   The sentence of excommunication is, by the law of this church, applicable to the following cases only :

1. To the case of a bishop or minister who has been degraded from his office ; in which case he may also be expelled from the Holy Communion in the discretion of the ecclesiastical authority, or court having jurisdiction.

Whenever a sentence of degradation is accompanied with a sentence of excommunication, a time for which the same shall continue, or terms upon which it shall cease, shall be expressed therein. In no case shall such latter sentence continue for more than two years.

It shall at any time within such two years, be lawful for any three Bishops of this Church to remove the sentence of excommunication, when passed upon a Bishop ; or to pronounce the terms and conditions of such sentence complied with, whereupon the same shall terminate ; and where the sentence has been pronounced upon a minister, the Ecclesiastical authority of the diocese shall have the like power. (a.)

(a.) A canon of the Scottish Church, drawn by Bishop White, in the year 1783, deserves notice, " If any presbyter or deacon, who shall have the misfortune to be deposed by his Bishop, do presume to perform any part of the sacred office, or to gather a separate or schismatical congregation, he shall be excommunicated. And if any clergyman shall take upon him to countenance such presbyter or deacon in their schismatical separation, he shall be suspended from the exercise of his holy functions for such space as his Bishop shall see fit. And such of the laity as shall venture to adhere to the deposed presbyter or deacon, either in worship or other sacred administrations, shall not be allowed to partake of any church ordinances until they are reconciled again, and received by the Bishop of the diocese."

2. To the sentence of suspension from communion which may be pronounced by a presbyter upon a layman, according to the rubrics and canons of the church. (a.)

Notice of the sentence of suspension or degradation of a minister or bishop shall be sent to the Ecclesiastical authority of every diocese of this church. And such authority shall cause notice of the same to be read to the congregations of such diocese, by the respective ministers thereof. 8

A copy of such sentence shall be sent to the accused, and another to the vestry of the parish or congregations, with which he may be canonically connected.

The sentence to be pronounced after a judicial enquiry in either of the modes contained in this canon, shall be as follows, to wit : 9

The sentence for a violation of a constitution or canon not involving immorality, shall be only admonition, or suspension for a limited and definite time. The sentence for teaching doctrine inconsistent with that of the church, but not amounting to heresy, shall always be suspension until the false doctrine is recanted ; the sentence for heresy shall be, for the first offence, suspension until the party shall recant the heresy ; and for the second, degradation ; the sentence for schism shall be degradation. The sentence for other offences shall be either admonition, suspension for a limited and definite time, or to be determined by some event or some act of the suspended party mentioned in the sentence, or degration.

(a.) See Hoffman's Law of the Church, 435.

APPENDIX.

Note I.—Page 9.

In looking over Mr. Selden's Treatise De Synedriis Ebræorum, I find it stated, that several of the fathers were of the opinion that the Elders of the Council of Jerusalem were the seventy, or some of them, commissioned by our Lord.

This is a striking and very interesting view of the subject. It has important bearings, besides the one now in question.

The first place in Scripture in which Elders are mentioned in connection with the Christian Church is in Acts, chap. 11, v. 30. After the prophecy of a famine, the Disciples at Antioch sent relief for the Brethren in Judea, to the Elders, by the hands of Barnabas and Saul. (*a*.)

They are next mentioned in the 14th chapter, v. 23. " When Paul and Barnabas had returned to Lystria, Iconium, and An- tioch, they ordained them Elders in every city."

Then in a chronological succession, is the text in question in this 15th chapter of Acts, shewing the Elders to have been members of the Council.

Again, when Paul arrived at Jerusalem, " he went with us unto James, and all the Elders were present." (ch. 21, v. 18.)

It is then certain, that Elders resided at Jerusalem, a distinct, ackr.owledged, official body. It is, I believe, conceded by all writers, that the Elders of the New Testament were of the Priestly order.

In a few cases, in which the term " Elders " occurs, it seems to be used as indicating merely persons seniors in age ; but ordinarily it denotes a distinct body of men.

Now I believe there are but three places in the New Testament

(*a*.) The supposition I have met with, that these were the Jewish Elders is of all things, the most improbable.

in which the ordination of Elders is mentioned ; one in the 14th chapter of Acts, where Paul and Barnabas ordained them Elders in every city ; and the other in the Epistle to Titus, directing him to ordain Elders. And the third in the injunction to Timothy to lay hands suddenly on no man.

It follows that the Elders at Jerusalem in the council were either ordained by the apostles, of which we have no record, or held a distinct and sacred office, by virtue of a commission from the Saviour.

Our Lord communicated a portion of his authority and offices to two classes of followers ; to the twelve apostles, and to the seventy disciples. The first commission to the apostles was in the thirty-first year, and that to the seventy in the thirty-second year of his abode on earth.

The apostles were superior in dignity to the seventy ; superior in the extent of authority delegated, and in its permanence.

They were first appointed. Although there was no difference as to the extent of their respective powers when first delegated, yet those of the apostles were afterwards renewed and increased ; while the seventy, having executed their office and returned, were never recommissioned, nor are they again mentioned by our Lord. The seventy were restricted to the cities and places which our Lord intended to visit ; the apostles were sent to all nations.

Yet the seventy remained distinguished by some supernatural power and gifts ; the power to tread upon serpents ; nothing was to hurt them, and their names were written in heaven.

From the time of the commission given to the seventy, to the meeting of the council of Jerusalem, was about a year.

That a large number of these should remain at Jerusalem ; that the commission once bestowed, and the spiritual sacredness assured them, should give them consideration and influence, may with all reason be assumed. Their presence in the council may be presumed with every probability of truth ; and we thus have a reasonable explanation of their existence and office at Jerusalem as a distinct class, without the trace of an ordination ; and we also find a practical bearing, as well as a poetic beauty, in the figment of Origen, that the apostles were like the twelve fountains of Elm, and the seventy, the palm trees upon their margins.

Note 2, *p.* 11.

There is a passage in the old Testament somewhat analogous. And Moses, *with the Elders of Israel*, commanded the people, saying, " Keep all the commandments which I this day command you."

In the work of Sir Peter King, it was insisted that the narrative of the Council of Antioch, which condemned Samontanus, proved that the laity were present, or represented in it. He relies upon a passage in the Synodical Epistle.

Sclater (Original Draft, pp. 74, 287, 289,) has, I think, fully refuted this view, and if we turn to the record of that council, every doubt must be removed.

The council was held in the year 272. The epistle is directed to Dyonisius, the Roman Pontiff, and to the other associate (Collegas) Bishops, from the second council of Antioch. It was thus. " To Dyonisius Maximus and all other associate Bishops, Presbyters and Deacons of the whole globe, and to the universal Catholic Church—Helenus and Hermanus and Theophilus, and all the other Bishops, Priests and Deacons, who dwell in our city and neighboring regions, and *churches of God* which are among us, to our beloved brothers' health."

Can it be imagined that such a phrase implies a co-ordinate power in every lay member of the church who might have been present ?

The records of the Councils which we find in the Corpus Canonici, and in Van Espen, as well as in the larger works of Mansi, so far as I have been able to examine them, tend strongly to prove that the actual power was in Bishops, or in Bishops and clergy alone, according to the character of the Synod. Take, for example, the sixth Council of Carthage, held in the year 419. Two hundred and seventeen Bishops were present, and the record assumes the form of a journal. Faustinus, Episcopus dixit—Placet ut, &c.—Ab universis Episcopis dictum est, placet, &c.—Aurelius Episcopus dixit, &c.—Ab universis Episcopis, &c. In this manner are the canons of this council passed—a suggestion by a Bishop, and a response by all or some.

I observe, in the interesting work of Hercher, which the Rev. Mr. Cox has done us the favor of publishing, that he cites the canon of the fourth Council of Carthage (A. D. 385) thus—irrita erit sententia Episcopi nisi clericorum *Sententia* confirmeretur.

But this is a mistake. The clause of the canon is—Episcopus nullius causam audiat *absque presentia* suorum clericorum; alioquin irrita erit sententia Episcopi, nisi clericorum *presentia* confirmeretur. I quote it from Van Espen, (Sec. 1, Tit. E.) cap. 4, vol. 1, p. 44, and also from the Corpus Canonici Decreti Pars 2d, p. 260.

I observe, also, in an article published in the True Catholic of October, 1852, a reference to a letter of the Rev. Edward Churton, from which it appears that the translation of passage in question, as to the members of the Council of Jerusalem, has been the subject of much learned critical discussion.

Of this I presume not to judge; but I have assumed, that the received translation is the true one; that the term Presbyters is not an adjective to Brethren, but that in the letter Missive, each order is distinct.

The question really comes to this—whether the form of this letter can controvert the strength of evidence which shews, that the actual power was in the Apostles and Elders.

In the Church Journal (*a*) is a letter of a Mr. Keble, taken from an English paper, in which he concludes that the question was decided at Antioch; and that the Apostles went up to Jerusalem only to obtain a more authoritative sanction for the decision. (*b*)

(*a*) Printed in New York, number for April, 1853.

(*b*) It becomes every son of the Church in every land, when he has occasion to mention the name of Keble, to proffer the tribute of his warm respect. Thousands of hearts in our Western world have been touched with deep emotion, perhaps "to fine issues," by the rich melody of his solemn strains—by the influences of poetry, whose spirit is so truly pictured in the following exquisite lines:

> "The blackbird's song at even-tide,
> And hers, who gay ascends,
> Filling the heavens far and wide,
> Are sweet. But none so blends,
> As thine,
> With calm decay, and peace divine."

But this does not seem warranted by the text. Certainly the apostles did not decide the matter judicially at Antioch. That they could have done so, is undeniable. Why they did not, is a point well deserving inquiry. The observations of Mr. Keble suggest one reason. It was desirable that the decision, of the most important question in its bearings, which had as yet arisen in the Church, should be made in the most authoritative manner.

Another reason may be offered. At that period the apostles had not established themselves in distinct portions of the Christian field, nor matured separate dioceses. A principle of itineracy still prevailed.—Jerusalem was the centre of the power and influence of the church. There was the collective body of apostles and elders, as is proven by the texts above quoted, and others. (a)

I observe also that the Rev. Mr. Churton has answered the letter of Mr. Keble, and states his conviction that the laity shared in the council at Jerusalem, and were present, and participating in future councils.

It is not for me to oppose my imperfect knowledge to that of a divine so eminent ; but I had supposed that after the work of Sclater the question as to future councils was at an end.(b) Nor can I pretend to speak of the comparative authority due to canonists. But I have had very frequently to examine Van Espen ; and as a lawyer, I greatly admire the complete manner in which his topics are discussed. He lays down a rule ; cites canons and authorities to establish it—quotes what is against it ; the glosses and corrolaries from the rule ; and then makes his own summing up. Now his works abound with proofs of the entire ultimate authority of Bishops in all judicial matters, and of the fact that the actual authority in councils provincial vested in the Bishops, and in Diocesan Synods, in Bishop and clergy. De Censuris Ecclesiasticis, Tractatus Historico-Canonicus, p. 41, § 5. Apud. Vol. 2. Juris Ecc. Un.

(a) The apostles which were at Jerusalem sent Peter and John to the proselytes in Samaria. (Acts 8, 14.) And the Church at Jerusalem sent forth Barnabas to Antioch. (Ibid. 11—21.

So the Epistle in Acts xvi—that some had gone from us who have troubled you, &c.—"to whom we gave no such commandment." See also Barrow on the Supre. macy, p. 129.

(b) Draft of a Primitive Church.

Part III, Tit. 10 § 6, cap. 2, citing 3d Council of Carthage can. 9. Council of Chalcedon canon 9. De Repagulo nimiæ Exemptionum, &c. Tome 2, page 298. De Autoitate Sacrorum Canonum, cap. II. De Synodis Diocesanis, Jur. Ecc. Un Part I. Tit. 18, cap. 1, De Synodis Provincialibus. Ibid. Tit. 20, &c.

The record of the Diocesan Synod of Moguntium, A. D. 1022, is instructive. (Van Espen, Jur. Ecc. Un. Part I. cap. 2.) It is stated that all the assembled presbyters first enter and seat themselves according to the order of their ordination; then enter the approved deacons; then the laity of good conversation are introduced; and lastly the Bishop, or in case of necessity his Vicar.

The Bishop then salutes those present, and recites several prayers; and then all but the presbyters and certain proper clerics are directed to retire.

On the first day of the Synod, the cases of the clergy are heard, and on the second if these are finished, the complaints of the laity are heard.

See also the records of Diocesan Synods in England in the Bishop of Exeter's address in the acts of the Synod of Exeter, 1852; and also a learned article of Dean Newman, in a speech delivered in the Diocese of Capetown, Apud Synodalia for May, p. 421. In this the participation of the laity is supported with learning and ability. (a)

I confess nothing I have met with appears to approach a proof of the laity, either at Jerusalem, or in any of the early councils, having anything like a concurrent power in legislating for the church. That their approbation of what had been decided was sought, and wisely sought, is undoubted. And this it seems to me was the extent of their office, and best accords with the current of authority.

One remark more. Can it be imagined that immediately upon proselytes being admitted to church communion by the apostles, or their immediate successors, they were allowed to share in the government and legislation of the church? If not, then if ever admitted, they were so upon the principle of tried fitness and fidelity in a body, or upon the principle of selection from such a

(a) See also a paper addressed by the Glasgow Church Institute to the Primus and Bishop of the Church of Scotland.—*Synodalia note.*

body. None but the rulers of the church could have power to judge of this fitness, or make this selection. That settles the whole question in my judgment.

I have been surprised, however, to learn, that some have viewed this subject, as if the introduction of the laity in councils was unlawful. Most certainly, unless the Gospel had expressly, or by inevitable inference forbidden it, the matter is one of conventional arrangement with those who possess the power. On the theory that this power resided with the bishops, united to a certain extent with their clergy, it seems to me the clearest of all propositions, that they may share the power with the other members of Christ's body, supposing even that they may not utterly rob themselves of it. Let it be ever remembered that this participation of authority is not in things divine; but in things temporal, which minister to things divine.

In the discussions upon this subject we often find the representation of the laity spoken of as effected by the presence of princes in person, or through their commissioners. (a.) Lord Hardwicke, in his celebrated argument in Middleton's case, takes the same view, as connected with the ages of the emperors and despotic princes; but rejects it as applicable to the laity of England. I substitute for what I had written on this subject, the following admirable observations of the Rev. Dr. Seabury, which have within a few hours met my eye :—

" In such a state of things, the lay power and influence which it had been the purpose of the Reformation to assert and vindicate, passed to the people in name but not in fact; the crown and parliament who exercised the legitimate lay element of the church, having almost as little sympathy with the people, as the Pope and his cardinals who had absorbed and extinguished that element; and the people, as a body, being under the one as under the other, effectually shut out from the just sphere of their influence in the election of church officers, the management of church property, and the enactment of church laws." (b.)

(a.) See among others the Letter of the Rev. Ed. Churton, Synodalia, No. 7, p. 420.

(b.) Continuity of the Church, &c. The True Catholic of August 1853, received as these pages were going through the press, contains an excellent summary of the learning upon the share of Princes in the Councils, taken from the Scottish Ecclesiastical Journal.

I apprehend that since the adoption of the absolute veto in the House of Bishops, the General Council of our Church presents the system in the best form possible ; in which the great advantages of lay assistance and concurrence are united with the great principle of a Diocesan Episcopacy. And in our Diocesan Conventions, the vote by orders secures to the clergy an effectual power and safeguard.

Note III.—Page 18.

Presentment :

    To, &c.,

        do present the Rev.   for trial upon the following charges and allegations :

That the said the Rev.   a minister of this Church, of the order of priests, and canonically resident within the diocese of New York, has been guilty of a violation of the constitution of this Church, contrary to the provisions of the laws of this Church, and particularly of the 27th canon of the General Convention of 1832 and the second section thereof. In support of which charge these presenters state and allege—

1. That in and by the seventh article of the constitution of this Church, it is provided : That no person shall be ordained until he shall have subscribed the following declaration : " I do believe the holy Scriptures of the Old and New Testament to be the Word of God, and to contain all things necessary to salvation ; and I do solemnly engage to conform to the doctrine and worship of the Protestant Episcopal Church in the United States."

2. That in and by the 8th article of such constitution, adopted by a General Convention, it was provided, that a Book of Common Prayer, administration of the Sacraments, and other rites and ceremonies of the Church, articles of religion, and a form and manner of making, ordaining and consecrating bishops, priests and deacons, when established by this or future General Convention, shall be used in the Protestant Episcopal Church in those dioceses which shall have adopted this constitution."

3. That the diocese of New York has adopted such constitution.

4. That the bishops, clergy, and laity of the Protestant Episcopal Church in the United States of America in convention, held on the 16th day of October in that year, 1789, did ratify and estab-

lish the Book of Common Prayer in the manner following, to wit: " This convention, having in their present session set forth ' a Book of Common Prayer and administration of the Sacraments, and other rites and ceremonies of the Church,' do hereby establish the said book ; and they declare it to be the liturgy of this Church, and require that it be received as such by all the members of the same,' which book, it was declared, should be in use from and after the 1st day of October, in the year of our Lord, 1790," which said Book of Common Prayer, as above mentioned, did remain established by authority, aforesaid, at the time of the commission of the ecclesiastical officers hereafter mentioned.

5. That the bishops, clergy and laity of the Protestant Episcopal Church in the United States of America, did, in General Convention, in the month of September, in the year of our Lord 1792, declare and establish " the form and manner of making, ordaining and consecrating bishops, priests and deacons. That as part of the form and manner so established, was an order or office, entitled " the form or manner of ordering priests, in and by which it is among other things ordered and directed, that such persons as do come to be admitted priests shall answer plainly to those things which the bishop, in the name of God and his Church, shall demand of them ; and that the bishop shall, among other things, demand of him thus : ' Will you give your faithful diligence always so to minister the doctrine and sacraments, and the discipline of Christ, as the Lord hath commanded, and as this Church has received the same according to the commandments of God, so that you may teach the people committed to your care and charge with all diligence to keep and observe the same ?" to which demand such person is to answer : " I will do so, by the help of the Lord."

6. That the bishops, clergy and laity of the Protestant Episcopal Church in the United States of America, in General Convention held on the 12th day of September, in the year 1801, did establish and declare articles of religion as held by this Church.

7. And these presenters further state and allege, that the said the Rev.   was, at the time of the commission of the ecclesiastical offences hereinafter set forth, and before and since a minis ter of this Church, of the order of priests. That he, the said   had been duly admitted to the order of priests, and had thereupon taken and subscribed the promise and engagement set

forth and contained in the seventh article of the constitution of this Church hereinbefore mentioned.

8. That the said   was duly ordained a priest under and according to the office entitled " the form and manner of ordering priests," before referred to ; and thereupon did openly and advisedly take, pronounce, and declare the promise and vow hereinbefore stated as prescribed to be taken, and made upon receiving the holy orders of a priest, in and by such office.

9. And these Presenters further allege and submit, that it is the doctrine of the Protestant Episcopal Church in the United States, and the doctrine of Christ, as this church has received the same, that auricular or private confession of sins to a priest is at no time or place, or under any circumstances, allowable ; *except*, that under and according to the office of the church, entitled, " The order for the administration of the Lord's Supper, or Holy Communion," a person desirous of receiving the same, may open his grief to a minister for the purpose of such godly advice and counsel as may tend to quiet his conscience ; *and except* that in case of a person condemned to die, a full confession of sins, and a particular confession of the sin for which he is condemned to die, may be made to a priest, under and according to the office entitled, " Of the Visitation of Prisoners," contained in such Book of Common Prayer ; *and except*, that in times of contagious sickness or disease, when none of the parish or neighbours can be gotten to communicate with the sick in their houses, for fear of the infection, the minister may with such person alone, make the general confession of sins set forth in the said order for the administration of the Lord's Supper or Holy Communion, as the same is allowed and directed in that part of the said Book of Common Prayer, entitled, " The Communion of the Sick."

10. That it is the doctrine of the Protestant Episcopal Church in the United States, and the doctrine of Christ, as this church has received the same, that auricular or private confession to a priest, with a view or for the purpose of obtaining a private absolution of sins, is wholly unlawful and unwarranted, *except*, that in the case of a person condemned to die, upon a full confession of sins, and a particular confession of the sin for which he is condemned, and under the provisions in the office " cf the Visitation of Prisoners," the priest shall declare to him the pardoning

mercy of God in the form which is used in the Communion service ; *and except*, that in times of contagious sickness, &c., (as in
the last clause of article 8, next preceding, adding after the words
" Holy Communion,") with the view and for the purpose of the
minister communicating alone with such person ; in which case the
declaration of absolution or remission of sins, set forth in such
order, may be made; as is allowed and directed in that part of
the said Book of Common Prayer.

11. That it is *not* the doctrine of the Protestant Episcopal
Church in the United States, but on the contrary is repugnant
thereto, that auricular or private confession to a priest, may, at any
convenient time and place, be lawfully used for the soul's health
and growth in spiritual grace.

12. That it is not the doctrine of the Protestant Episcopal
Church in the United States, but on the contrary repugnant
thereto, that auricular or private confession to a priest, with a
view or for the purpose of obtaining absolution of sins, is at all
convenient times and places lawful, and useful for the soul's
health and growth in spiritual grace.

NEVERTHELESS, as these Presenters state and allege, the said
the Reverend   , in violation of his said engagement
and subscription and of the constitution of this church (and also
in violation of his ordination vow taken as aforesaid, hath held,
taught, preached, or inculcated, divers dectrines respecting auricular confession and priestly absolution, as next herein set forth.

2. That in the City of   , and within   from
the date of this presentment, he hath held, taught, preached, or
inculcated the doctrine that auricular or private confession of sins
to a priest was, at any and all convenient times and places lawful
and expedient, and useful for the soul's health.

That in the City of   , and within
from the date of this presentment, he hath held and taught,
preached or inculcated that auricular or private confession to a
priest, for the purpose or with a view of thereupon obtaining absolution at his hands, was at all convenient times and places lawful,
and useful for the health of the soul.

14. That at the place aforesaid, and within the period aforesaid, he hath held, taught, preached, or inculcated, that auricular

or private confession of sins to a priest was lawful and according to the doctrine of this church, at other times, and on other occasions than as mentioned and set forth in the " order for the administration of the Lord's Supper or Holy Communion," or in the order or office for the visitation of prisoners, or in the order or office entitled " The Communion of the Sick," all such orders or offices being parts of and contained in the said Book of Common Prayer.

Wherefore, we, the undersigned, do present the said for trial, and censure upon the charges and allegations herein contained.

NOTE.—I beg to repeat that I do not pretend to say whether the allegations, if made out, amount to the holding erroneous doctrine. My private opinion is of course of no moment. Nor do I presume to say whether Mr. Prescott's letter or the evidence proved that he held them. I only urge that if, as the court appear to have thought, he held such opinions, a presentment could be framed, as our law now stands, on the basis of their being doctrines, contrary to those of the church, and no objection to jurisdiction could be taken.

PRESENTMENT ADAPTED TO THE CASE OF MR. HEAD.

Note IV., Page 18.

(SEE 3 CURTIES REPORTS, 567.)

[The charge, and the first eight allegations or articles of the preceding presentment, would, with slight variations, be applicable to this.] Then proceed.

9th. And these presenters further allege and submit, that by the Ecclesiastical law of this church, whatsoever portions of such Book of Common Prayer do relate to the doctrine and worship of such church is, and of right ought to be avowed, sustained, and declared as agreeable to Holy Scripture, and warranted thereby.

That whatsoever portions of such Book do relate to the doctrine of this church, do contain the doctrine of Christ as received by this church.

That no portion of such Book doth contain any strange or erroneous doctrine—but that the same is taken out of Holy Scripture, or may be sufficiently proven thereby.

10. Nevertheless, as these presenters allege, the said   in the month of   in the year of our Lord   wrote and published, or caused to be published, within the diocese of   to wit in a certain newspaper called the &c., dated the, &c., a letter entitled " a view, &c.," in which letter the said   advisedly affirmed and maintained, that the " Catechism," the " order of Baptism," and the " order of Confirmation " in the Book of Common Prayer, contain erroneous and strange doctrines, and wherein he also advisedly affirmed and maintained other positions in derogation and depravation of the said Book of Common Prayer contrary to the Ecclesiastical law of this church, and against its peace and unity.

11. And these presenters further allege, that in the said letter mentioned in the next preceding article, are contained the following passages :—" I do hereby decline and refuse to give any countenance to the office of Confirmation as it is now used, and instead of recommending the perusal and reperusal of that service to the young persons of this parish, I warn them all, young, old, and middle aged, to beware, in the name of God, of the erroneous and strange doctrine which it contains."

This will suffice.

Note v. page 18.

SKETCH OF A PRESENTMENT IN THE GORHAM CASE.

[The first eight articles of the Presentment No. IV.]

X.—1. That it is the doctrine of this church, to be read in, or warranted by such standards thereof, that all unbaptised infants are subject to the condemnation of the first man, and that original sin passed over to them, from which they must be cleansed, in order to be saved.

13

2. That it is the doctrine of this church that all baptised infants, baptised according to the ministration for the Baptism of Infants, do obtain remission of original sin, in baptism, by virtue of God's grace, procured through the atonement of the Lord Jesus Christ.

3. That it is the doctrine of this church that all infants baptised according to the ministration for the Baptism of Infants, as appointed by this church, and dying before the commission of actual sin, are undoubtedly saved.

4. That it is the doctrine of this church that all infants baptiseed according to the office before mentioned, and dying before the commission of actual sin are undoubtedly saved, by the grace of God, procured by the atonement of the Lord Jesus, and conferred in baptism.

5. That it is the doctrine of this church that all infants baptised according to the office aforesaid are regenerated, and made children of God, and inheritors of the kingdom of heaven.

6. That it is the doctrine of this church that all infants baptised according to the office aforesaid are regenerated, and made children of God and inheritors of the kingdom of heaven, by virtue of the grace of God, procured by the atonement of the Lord Jesus, and conferred in baptism.

7. That it is *not* the doctrine of this church, that infants cannot be worthy recipients of the rite of baptism, unless by a prevenient act of God's grace, the guilt of original sin had been taken away.

8. That it is *not* the doctrine of this church that original sin is not remitted to any infants, baptised according to the office aforesaid, in, by, or through baptism.

9. That it is *not* the doctrine of this church that no infant, baptised as aforesaid, doth receive any benefit from baptism except there hath been a prevenient act of grace, by which the original sin hath been done away, and the infant regenerated, and rendered worthy.

10. That it is *not* the doctrine of this church that such prevenient act of grace is not given to all infants, but only to some, and denied to others, according to the will of God.

XI. Nevertheless, that the said   doth hold, avow, declare, in writing, and inculcate, and at divers places, and at divers times within   months prior to the date hereof, hath held, avowed, declared in writing, and inculcated that—[a general statement of the holding, &c. the converse of the main propositions in article X.]

XII. And especially that the said   in a writing signed by him on or about the   day of   in reply to certain questions to him administered, did make answer, state and declare as follows, to wit :

Being asked whether, &c., he replied : " Our church holds, and I hold, that no spiritual grace is conferred in baptism, except to worthy recipients ; and in infants are by nature unworthy recipients, being born in sin and the children of wrath, they cannot receive any benefit from baptism, except there shall have been a prevenient act of grace to make them worthy."

And being further interrogated as follows : " In your answer you say," (respecting the above.) " Do you mean that a prevenient act of grace is necessary to enable infants being born in sin, and the children of wrath to receive any benefit from baptism ?" To which, he the said   did answer—" I do."

And the said   did further state and declare as follows : " In fact the new nature must have been possessed by those who receive baptism rightly, and therefore possessed before the seal was affixed."

[These passages and those in which the limitation of the gift of the prevenient grace to such as God wills, are too numerous and long to quote. The above will, I believe, suffice to show the leading tenet of Mr. Gorham.]

The following, I believe, is an accurate synopsis of Mr. Gorham's positions.

That neither adults nor infants can receive any benefit from Baptism, unless they are first made worthy recipients thereof.

That in the case of infants, the existence in them of original sin renders them unworthy recipients. Such original sin must be removed before they can become worthy, and partake of any benefit in baptism.

This original sin is taken away by an act of prevenient grace, which comes before baptism, and is essential to make it efficacious.

No regeneration, or remission of original sin, is effected in or by

Baptism for infants. The prevenient grace must have been previously bestowed.

This prevenient grace does not necessarily attend or is bestowed upon every infant brought to be baptised. To some it is given and to some denied; and this gift or refusal is according to the unknown will of God.

It is not denied that the grace may be, and is given, at the moment of baptism. [Mr. Gorham's propositions logically require that this should still precede the rite if even by the minutest fraction of time.]

" The church holds, and I hold that *if such infants* die before they commit actual sin, they *must* have been regenerated by an act of grace prevenient to their baptism, in order to render them worthy recipients of that sacrament. (Answer 19.)

At the first perusal of this answer, every one would probably conclude, that Mr. Gorham held that all baptised infants were saved, and then one portion of his alleged error or heresy would have been met; for whether he held that the remission or regeneration was always given in baptism, or that the previous grace was always conferred upon those brought to be baptised, would, so far as the doctrine of the salvation of the infant was concerned, be immaterial.

But Mr. Gorham does not hold this, but rejects it. And it is not possible to render him consistent, unless by interpreting the words *such infants* to mean, infants who have been made worthy recipients of the sacrament; and to make them worthy, they must in his view have before received an act of grace.

Nothing can be more certain than that these opinions result in Predestination. Whether right or wrong, they are all wholly irreconcilable with the position that *all* baptised infants, dying before actual sin, are undoubtedly saved.

On the other side, as I understand it, what is asserted to be the doctrine of the church is this : that infants baptised are spiritually regenerated, absolved from original sin, and made children of God, through his grace, obtained by virtue of the atonement, and bestowed in baptism; so that all three concurring, and all three essential, the infant is undoubtedly saved.

Whether this is the doctrine of Scripture and the Church is not for me to say. But at least, a plain man may express his wonder how such a doctrine could ever be conceived as trenching upon the freeness of the gift of God, or derogating from the all sufficiency of the atonement.

Note 6.—Page 80.

The subject of this section was brought before the Convention of New York in 1853, in consequence of injunctions, and applications for injunctions, against the proceedings of Presenters and a Court, on various grounds, chiefly resulting in a want of jurisdiction. The applications failed, but were annoying and expensive. A committee of eminent members of the Convention made a report, the principal portions of which follow. There being no time to discuss it, and some objections arising, it was laid over. The remarks of some judicious persons were directed against the operation of so much of it as prohibited suits after an acquittal against malicious accusers.

Such objections deserve consideration, and the canon should be guarded also against a construction which prohibits the right to apply to the Civil Courts after sentence, so far as a question relative to property is concerned. Of course such tribunals will judge of the effect of a sentence on such rights, whether such a clause is inserted or not. But it seems unwise to prohibit this application by an ecclesiastical penalty.

The provision I suggest forbids the resort to a civil tribunal during the progress of a case, but leaves the remedies after sentence as they now exist.

It is true that in several early canons clerics charged with an ecclesiastical offence, were forbidden to carry the case to a secular tribunal;—and a similar rule was adopted in the Free Church of Scotland. (a) But this was at an early period altered, and recourse to the civil power was had, sometimes to enforce ecclesiastical judgments, often to redress ecclesiastical oppression, or error. Van Espen has written an elaborate tract upon this subject.

(a) North British Review—N

Tractatus De Recarsu ad Principem. He sums up the matter in the following words, comprising the sound and the prevailing doctrine of our most eminent tribunals upon the question. " If, then, one is cited before an incompetent tribunal, or has not been cited at all, or if the judge of that tribunal, otherwise competent, being lawfully challenged proceeds notwithstanding, or if he refuses to hear witnesses, to examine proofs, or to observe other rules of law, and thus pronounces sentence—this would be a manifest injustice,—one which would open the way to a recourse to the sovereign protection and support.

The Report referred to was in substance as follows—

After stating the formation of a Court for trial upon a presentment, and the objections taken by the accused, and the falling through of the Court, with the steps taken to form a new one, it proceeded : " ——— had commenced suits against the Presbyters who prosecuted him for libel, and had resorted to the Civil Courts to enjoin the Ecclesiastical Court from proceeding to the trial, and four of such suits are stated to be now pending. In a moral and religious aspect, this conduct is so scandalous to the institutions of the Church, so subversive of all principles of subordination and good faith, by which any community, society or association is bound and kept together, and so utterly destructive of all order, government and discipline, as to deserve the most severe animadversion, and the application of the most prompt remedies.

Your Committee consider that it is not only the right, but the bounden duty of every church organization, to cut off from connection with it, any member who disavows its authority, and seeks to supersede it by invoking the power of the secular tribunals. From the very nature of the relations of the member to his church, this must be an offence of the greatest magnitude ; it has all the characteristics of treason to his church, and must be dealt with, or the Church organization must dissolve from its inherent weakness."

The canon submitted was as follows :

In all cases in which an inquiry into the conduct of a minister of this diocese shall have been, or shall be directed, by the proper ecclesiastical authority thereof, any resort by such minister to the civil Courts, or to any Judge thereof, for the purpose of obstructing or preventing such inquiry; and any such resort for the recovery of any damages against the persons making such inquiry, in consequence of any report by them, or for the recovery of damages against them, or any presbyters, for making a regular presentment against any minister of the Diocese, or for any thing contained in such presentment; and any such resort for the purpose of obstructing or preventing, or staying any proceeding upon such presentment, shall be deemed disorderly conduct in such minister, for which on due presentment, trial, and conviction, he shall be admonished, suspended, or degraded from his office."

INDEX TO THE CANON.

GENERAL PROVISIONS.

CHAPTER II.—OF APPEALS.

▼

CHAPTER III.—OF THE TRIAL OF A BISHOP.

SECTION I.

Definition of Terms.

MISCELLANEOUS PROVISIONS.

SECTION I.

Of Witnesses refusing to testify, &c.

SECTION II.

Application to Civil Tribunals.

SECTION III.

Of Sentences.